Just The facts101

Textbook Key Facts

Just The

Bundle: Survey Of Economics

Table of Contents

Title Page

Copyright

Introduction to economics

Fundamental economics

Mathematical and quantitative methods

Microeconomics

Macroeconomics and monetary economics

Business economics

International economics

Index: Answers

Just The Facts101

Exam Prep for

Bundle: Survey Of Economics

Just The Facts101 Exam Prep is your link from
the textbook and lecture to your exams.

**Just The Facts101 Exam Preps are unauthorized and comprehensive reviews
of your textbooks.**

All material provided by CTI Publications (c) 2019

Textbook publishers and textbook authors do not participate in or contribute to these reviews.

Just The Facts101 Exam Prep

eAIN 459383

Introduction to economics

Prices and quantities have been described as the most directly observable attributes of goods produced and exchanged in a market economy. The theory of supply and demand is an organizing principle for explaining how prices coordinate the amounts produced and consumed.

:: Economics models ::

In economics, a model is a theoretical construct representing economic processes by a set of variables and a set of logical and/or quantitative relationships between them. The _____ is a simplified, often mathematical, framework designed to illustrate complex processes. Frequently, _____ s posit structural parameters. A model may have various exogenous variables, and those variables may change to create various responses by economic variables. Methodological uses of models include investigation, theorizing, and fitting theories to the world.

1. *Answer choices:*

(see index for correct answer)

- a. Baker cube
- b. Backwardness
- c. Economic model
- d. Keynesian cross

Guidance: level 1

:: Stock market ::

_____ is freedom from, or resilience against, potential harm caused by others. Beneficiaries of _____ may be of persons and social groups, objects and institutions, ecosystems or any other entity or phenomenon vulnerable to unwanted change by its environment.

2. *Answer choices:*

(see index for correct answer)

- a. Pattern day trader
- b. Blue chip
- c. Open outcry

- d. Security

Guidance: level 1

:: Microeconomics ::

In financial accounting, an _____ is any resource owned by the business. Anything tangible or intangible that can be owned or controlled to produce value and that is held by a company to produce positive economic value is an _____ . Simply stated, _____ s represent value of ownership that can be converted into cash . The balance sheet of a firm records the monetary value of the _____ s owned by that firm. It covers money and other valuables belonging to an individual or to a business.

Exam Probability: **Low**

3. *Answer choices:*

(see index for correct answer)

- a. Schedule delay
- b. Asset
- c. Economies of scope
- d. Reservation price

Guidance: level 1

:: Cartels ::

A _____ is a group of apparently independent producers whose goal is to increase their collective profits by means of price fixing, limiting supply, or other restrictive practices. _____ s typically control selling prices, but some are organized to control the prices of purchased inputs. Antitrust laws attempt to deter or forbid _____ s. A single entity that holds a monopoly by this definition cannot be a _____ , though it may be guilty of abusing said monopoly in other ways. _____ s usually occur in oligopolies, where there are a small number of sellers and usually involve homogeneous products.

Exam Probability: **Low**

4. *Answer choices:*

(see index for correct answer)

- a. Asian Racing Federation
- b. Phoebus cartel
- c. Cartel
- d. Two Airlines Policy

Guidance: level 1

:: Great Depression ::

The _____ was a severe worldwide economic depression that took place mostly during the 1930s, beginning in the United States. The timing of the _____ varied across nations; in most countries it started in 1929 and lasted until the late-1930s. It was the longest, deepest, and most widespread depression of the 20th century. In the 21st century, the _____ is commonly used as an example of how intensely the world's economy can decline.

5. *Answer choices:*

(see index for correct answer)

- a. Great Depression
- b. Great Compression
- c. Causes of the Great Depression
- d. Comparisons between the Great Recession and the Great Depression

Guidance: level 1

:: Market structure and pricing ::

_____ is a type of imperfect competition such that many producers sell products that are differentiated from one another and hence are not perfect substitutes. In _____ , a firm takes the prices charged by its rivals as given and ignores the impact of its own prices on the prices of other firms. In the presence of coercive government, _____ will fall into government-granted monopoly. Unlike perfect competition, the firm maintains spare capacity. Models of _____ are often used to model industries. Textbook examples of industries with market structures similar to _____ include restaurants, cereal, clothing, shoes, and service industries in large cities. The "founding father" of the theory of _____ is Edward Hastings Chamberlin, who wrote a pioneering book on the subject, Theory of _____ . Joan Robinson published a book The Economics of Imperfect Competition with a comparable theme of distinguishing perfect from imperfect competition.

6. *Answer choices:*

(see index for correct answer)

- a. Market share
- b. Monopolistic competition
- c. industry concentration
- d. Market concentration

Guidance: level 1

:: Interest rates ::

The concept of real interest rate is useful to account for the impact of inflation. In the case of a loan, it is this real interest that the lender effectively receives. For example, if the lender is receiving 8 percent from a loan and the inflation rate is also 8 percent, then the real rate of interest is zero: despite the increased nominal amount of currency received, the lender would have no monetary value benefit from such a loan because each unit of currency would get devaluated due to inflation by the same factor as the nominal amount gets increased.

Exam Probability: **High**

7. *Answer choices:*

(see index for correct answer)

- a. Rule of 78s
- b. Annual effective discount rate

- c. Coupon leverage
- d. Nominal interest rate

Guidance: level 1

:: Communism ::

In political and social sciences, _____ is the philosophical, social, political, and economic ideology and movement whose ultimate goal is the establishment of the communist society, which is a socioeconomic order structured upon the common ownership of the means of production and the absence of social classes, money, and the state.

Exam Probability: **Medium**

8. *Answer choices:*

(see index for correct answer)

- a. Communism
- b. Assemblywomen
- c. Living Marxism
- d. Husakism

Guidance: level 1

:: Production economics ::

In economics, _____ is the decrease in the marginal output of a production process as the amount of a single factor of production is incrementally increased, while the amounts of all other factors of production stay constant.

Exam Probability: **Medium**

9. *Answer choices:*

(see index for correct answer)

- a. Division of work
- b. Fragmentation
- c. Diminishing returns
- d. Indirect cost

Guidance: level 1

:: Taxation ::

A _____ is a reduction in the rate of tax charged by a government. The immediate effects of a _____ are a decrease in the real income of the government and an increase in the real income of those whose tax rates have been lowered. Due to the perceived benefit in growing real incomes among tax payers, politicians have sought to claim their proposed tax credits as _____ s. In the longer term, however, the macroeconomic effects of a _____ are generally not predictable because they depend on how the taxpayers use their additional income and how the government adjusts to its reduced income.

10. *Answer choices:*

(see index for correct answer)

- a. Tax cut
- b. Ad valorem tax
- c. Tax law
- d. Dual income tax

Guidance: level 1

:: Corporate finance ::

The _____ of a corporation is all of the shares into which ownership of the corporation is divided. In American English, the shares are commonly known as " _____ s". A single share of the _____ represents fractional ownership of the corporation in proportion to the total number of shares. This typically entitles the _____ holder to that fraction of the company's earnings, proceeds from liquidation of assets , or voting power, often dividing these up in proportion to the amount of money each _____ holder has invested. Not all _____ is necessarily equal, as certain classes of _____ may be issued for example without voting rights, with enhanced voting rights, or with a certain priority to receive profits or liquidation proceeds before or after other classes of shareholders.

Exam Probability: **Low**

11. *Answer choices:*

(see index for correct answer)

- a. Earnings call
- b. Management buyout
- c. Reverse greenshoe
- d. Stock

Guidance: level 1

:: Economics laws ::

The _____ is a fundamental principle of economic theory which states that, keeping other factors constant, an increase in price results in an increase in quantity supplied. In other words, there is a direct relationship between price and quantity: quantities respond in the same direction as price changes. This means that producers are willing to offer more of a product for sale on the market at higher prices by increasing production as a way of increasing profits.

Exam Probability: **Low**

12. *Answer choices:*

(see index for correct answer)

- a. Law of increasing costs
- b. Law of supply
- c. Laws of costs
- d. Laws of returns

:: Demand ::

_____ is the quantity of a good that consumers are willing and able to purchase at various prices during a given period of time.

Exam Probability: **Medium**

13. *Answer choices:*

(see index for correct answer)

- a. Demand
- b. demand schedule
- c. price elastic
- d. Effective demand

:: Export ::

An _____ in international trade is a good or service produced in one country that is bought by someone in another country. The seller of such goods and services is an _____ er; the foreign buyer is an importer.

14. *Answer choices:*

(see index for correct answer)

- a. Export
- b. Export hay
- c. Live export

Guidance: level 1

:: International economics ::

In finance, an _____ is the rate at which one currency will be exchanged for another. It is also regarded as the value of one country's currency in relation to another currency. For example, an interbank _____ of 114 Japanese yen to the United States dollar means that ¥114 will be exchanged for each US$1 or that US$1 will be exchanged for each ¥114. In this case it is said that the price of a dollar in relation to yen is ¥114, or equivalently that the price of a yen in relation to dollars is $1/114.

Exam Probability: **Medium**

15. *Answer choices:*

(see index for correct answer)

- a. European Monetary System
- b. Exchange rate

- c. Trade barrier
- d. Brazilian disease

Guidance: level 1

:: World Wide Web ::

_____ LLC is an American multinational technology company that specializes in Internet-related services and products, which include online advertising technologies, search engine, cloud computing, software, and hardware. It is considered one of the Big Four technology companies, alongside Amazon, Apple and Facebook.

Exam Probability: **High**

16. *Answer choices:*

(see index for correct answer)

- a. Web typography
- b. Google
- c. Lost in hyperspace
- d. SPDY

Guidance: level 1

:: Generally Accepted Accounting Principles ::

_____ is the principled guide to action taken by the administrative executive branches of the state with regard to a class of issues, in a manner consistent with law and institutional customs.

Exam Probability: **High**

27. *Answer choices:*

(see index for correct answer)

- a. Cameralism
- b. Slapsoftware
- c. Public policy
- d. Secretariat

Guidance: level 1

:: Political economy ::

In economics, _____ , or recession-inflation, is a situation in which the inflation rate is high, the economic growth rate slows, and unemployment remains steadily high. It presents a dilemma for economic policy, since actions intended to lower inflation may exacerbate unemployment, and vice versa.

Exam Probability: **Low**

28. *Answer choices:*

(see index for correct answer)

- a. Communal ownership
- b. Political economy of climate change
- c. Stagflation
- d. State ownership

Guidance: level 1

:: Competition (economics) ::

_____ arises whenever at least two parties strive for a goal which cannot be shared: where one's gain is the other's loss .

Exam Probability: **High**

29. *Answer choices:*
(see index for correct answer)

- a. Suggested retail price
- b. Regulatory competition
- c. Level playing field
- d. Blindspots analysis

Guidance: level 1

:: Monetary economics ::

The general _____ is a hypothetical daily measure of overall prices for some set of goods and services , in an economy or monetary union during a given interval , normalized relative to some base set. Typically, the general _____ is approximated with a daily price index, normally the Daily CPI. The general _____ can change more than once per day during hyperinflation.

Exam Probability: **Low**

30. *Answer choices:*

(see index for correct answer)

- a. bank reserves
- b. Inside money
- c. Cumulative process
- d. Lucas islands model

Guidance: level 1

:: National accounts ::

A _____ is monetary compensation paid by an employer to an employee in exchange for work done. Payment may be calculated as a fixed amount for each task completed , or at an hourly or daily rate , or based on an easily measured quantity of work done.

31. *Answer choices:*

(see index for correct answer)

- a. Gross state product
- b. Personal income
- c. Wage
- d. Compensation of employees

Guidance: level 1

:: Industrial Revolution ::

The _____ , now also known as the First _____ , was the transition to new manufacturing processes in Europe and the US, in the period from about 1760 to sometime between 1820 and 1840. This transition included going from hand production methods to machines, new chemical manufacturing and iron production processes, the increasing use of steam power and water power, the development of machine tools and the rise of the mechanized factory system. The _____ also led to an unprecedented rise in the rate of population growth.

Exam Probability: **High**

32. *Answer choices:*

(see index for correct answer)

- a. Coke

- b. Burden Iron Works
- c. Industrial Revolution
- d. Grubb Family Iron Dynasty

Guidance: level 1

:: Official statistics ::

_____ is the exchange of capital, goods, and services across international borders or territories.

Exam Probability: **High**

33. *Answer choices:*

(see index for correct answer)

- a. Statistics department
- b. Department of Statistics
- c. United Nations System of National Accounts
- d. International Trade

Guidance: level 1

:: Sociocultural globalization ::

The _____ is the global system of interconnected computer networks that use the _____ protocol suite to link devices worldwide. It is a network of networks that consists of private, public, academic, business, and government networks of local to global scope, linked by a broad array of electronic, wireless, and optical networking technologies. The _____ carries a vast range of information resources and services, such as the inter-linked hypertext documents and applications of the World Wide Web, electronic mail, telephony, and file sharing.

Exam Probability: **Medium**

34. *Answer choices:*

(see index for correct answer)

- a. World population
- b. International organization
- c. Global elite
- d. Internet

Guidance: level 1

:: International macroeconomics ::

The balance of trade, commercial balance, or net exports , is the difference between the monetary value of a nation's exports and imports over a certain time period. Sometimes a distinction is made between a balance of trade for goods versus one for services. The balance of trade measures a flow of exports and imports over a given period of time. The notion of the balance of trade does not mean that exports and imports are "in balance" with each other.

35. *Answer choices:*

(see index for correct answer)

- a. net export
- b. Trade deficit
- c. net exports
- d. trade surplus

Guidance: level 1

:: Philosophy of science ::

A _____ is a proposed explanation for a phenomenon. For a _____ to be a scientific _____ , the scientific method requires that one can test it. Scientists generally base scientific hypotheses on previous observations that cannot satisfactorily be explained with the available scientific theories. Even though the words " _____ " and "theory" are often used synonymously, a scientific _____ is not the same as a scientific theory. A working _____ is a provisionally accepted _____ proposed for further research, in a process beginning with an educated guess or thought.

Exam Probability: **High**

36. *Answer choices:*

(see index for correct answer)

- a. Hypothesis
- b. Vienna Circle
- c. Operational definition
- d. Subjectivity

Guidance: level 1

:: Economics models ::

The _____ of income or _____ is a model of the economy in which the major exchanges are represented as flows of money, goods and services, etc. between economic agents. The flows of money and goods exchanged in a closed circuit correspond in value, but run in the opposite direction. The _____ analysis is the basis of national accounts and hence of macroeconomics.

Exam Probability: **High**

37. *Answer choices:*

(see index for correct answer)

- a. Neocolonial dependence
- b. Structural estimation
- c. Hourglass Federalism
- d. Circular flow

Guidance: level 1

:: Income distribution ::

In economics, _____ is how a nation's total GDP is distributed amongst its population. Income and its distribution have always been a central concern of economic theory and economic policy. Classical economists such as Adam Smith, Thomas Malthus, and David Ricardo were mainly concerned with factor _____ , that is, the distribution of income between the main factors of production, land, labour and capital. Modern economists have also addressed this issue, but have been more concerned with the distribution of income across individuals and households. Important theoretical and policy concerns include the balance between income inequality and economic growth, and their often inverse relationship.

Exam Probability: **High**

38. *Answer choices:*

(see index for correct answer)

- a. Income distribution
- b. Redistributive justice
- c. Factor income
- d. Winner-Take-All Politics

Guidance: level 1

:: Microeconomics ::

A _____ is a technical term in psychology, economics and philosophy usually used in relation to choosing between alternatives. For example, someone prefers A over B if they would rather choose A than B.

Exam Probability: **High**

39. *Answer choices:*

(see index for correct answer)

- a. Herfindahl index
- b. Returns to scale
- c. producer surplus
- d. Preference

Guidance: level 1

:: United States housing bubble ::

In economics, a _____ is a business cycle contraction when there is a general decline in economic activity. Macroeconomic indicators such as GDP , investment spending, capacity utilization, household income, business profits, and inflation fall, while bankruptcies and the unemployment rate rise. In the United Kingdom, it is defined as a negative economic growth for two consecutive quarters.

Exam Probability: **High**

40. *Answer choices:*

(see index for correct answer)

- a. Recession
- b. Hardest Hit Fund
- c. Cuyahoga Land Bank
- d. Speculative fever

Guidance: level 1

:: Rational choice theory ::

In economics, "_____" are model-consistent expectations, in that agents inside the model are assumed to "know the model" and on average take the model's predictions as valid. _____ ensure internal consistency in models involving uncertainty. To obtain consistency within a model, the predictions of future values of economically relevant variables from the model are assumed to be the same as that of the decision-makers in the model, given their information set, the nature of the random processes involved, and model structure. The _____ assumption is used especially in many contemporary macroeconomic models.

Exam Probability: **High**

41. *Answer choices:*

(see index for correct answer)

- a. Social Choice and Individual Values
- b. Ecological rationality

- c. An Introduction to Karl Marx
- d. Rational expectations

Guidance: level 1

:: Macroeconomics ::

A _____ is an event that suddenly increases or decreases the supply of a commodity or service, or of commodities and services in general. This sudden change affects the equilibrium price of the good or service or the economy's general price level.

Exam Probability: **High**

42. *Answer choices:*

(see index for correct answer)

- a. Business cycle accounting
- b. Supply shock
- c. Ordoliberalism
- d. Recursive competitive equilibrium

Guidance: level 1

:: Economics curves ::

In economics, a _____ is a graph of the costs of production as a function of total quantity produced. In a free market economy, productively efficient firms optimize their production process by minimizing cost consistent with each possible level of production, and the result is a _____ ; and profit maximizing firms use _____ s to decide output quantities. There are various types of _____ s, all related to each other, including total and average _____ s; marginal _____ s, which are equal to the differential of the total _____ s; and variable _____ s. Some are applicable to the short run, others to the long run.

Exam Probability: **Medium**

43. *Answer choices:*

(see index for correct answer)

- a. Expectation hypothesis
- b. Contract curve
- c. Marginal propensity to save
- d. Rahn curve

Guidance: level 1

:: Political economy ::

_____ is the study of production and trade and their relations with law, custom and government; and with the distribution of national income and wealth. As a discipline, _____ originated in moral philosophy, in the 18th century, to explore the administration of states' wealth, with "political" signifying the Greek word polity and "economy" signifying the Greek word "okonomie". The earliest works of _____ are usually attributed to the British scholars Adam Smith, Thomas Malthus, and David Ricardo, although they were preceded by the work of the French physiocrats, such as François Quesnay and Anne-Robert-Jacques Turgot.

Exam Probability: **High**

44. *Answer choices:*

(see index for correct answer)

- a. Probabilistic voting model
- b. Deep state
- c. Capital accumulation
- d. Political economy

Guidance: level 1

:: Warrants issued in Hong Kong Stock Exchange ::

The _____ is the official currency of 19 of the 28 member states of the _____ pean Union. This group of states is known as the _____ zone or _____ area, and counts about 343 million citizens as of 2019. The _____ is the second largest and second most traded currency in the foreign exchange market after the United States dollar. The _____ is divided into 100 cents.

Exam Probability: **Medium**

45. *Answer choices:*

(see index for correct answer)

- a. SPDR Gold Shares
- b. Sino-Ocean Land
- c. Lenovo
- d. Hysan Development Company Limited

Guidance: level 1

:: Innovation ::

_____ , technological development, technological achievement, or technological progress is the overall process of invention, innovation and diffusion of technology or processes. In essence, _____ covers the invention of technologies and their commercialization or release as open source via research and development , the continual improvement of technologies , and the diffusion of technologies throughout industry or society . In short, _____ is based on both better and more technology.

46. *Answer choices:*

(see index for correct answer)

- a. Technological innovation system
- b. Systematic inventive thinking
- c. Technological change
- d. Social shaping of technology

Guidance: level 1

:: Keynesian economics ::

_____ are a group of various macroeconomic theories about how in the short run – and especially during recessions – economic output is strongly influenced by aggregate demand . In the Keynesian view, named for British economist John Maynard Keynes, aggregate demand does not necessarily equal the productive capacity of the economy; instead, it is influenced by a host of factors and sometimes behaves erratically, affecting production, employment, and inflation.

47. *Answer choices:*

(see index for correct answer)

- a. We are all Keynesians now

- b. Keynesian economics
- c. A Treatise on Money
- d. Keynesian Revolution

Guidance: level 1

:: Unemployment ::

_____ is a form of involuntary unemployment caused by a mismatch between the skills that workers in the economy can offer, and the skills demanded of workers by employers . _____ is often brought about by technological changes that make the job skills of many workers obsolete.

Exam Probability: **Low**

48. *Answer choices:*

(see index for correct answer)

- a. Structural unemployment
- b. Unemployment Convention, 1919
- c. Overqualification
- d. Technological unemployment

Guidance: level 1

:: Microeconomics ::

In economics, _____ is the change in the total cost that arises when the quantity produced is incremented by one unit; that is, it is the cost of producing one more unit of a good. Intuitively, _____ at each level of production includes the cost of any additional inputs required to produce the next unit. At each level of production and time period being considered, _____ s include all costs that vary with the level of production, whereas other costs that do not vary with production are fixed and thus have no _____ . For example, the _____ of producing an automobile will generally include the costs of labor and parts needed for the additional automobile but not the fixed costs of the factory that have already been incurred. In practice, marginal analysis is segregated into short and long-run cases, so that, over the long run, all costs become marginal. Where there are economies of scale, prices set at _____ will fail to cover total costs, thus requiring a subsidy. _____ pricing is not a matter of merely lowering the general level of prices with the aid of a subsidy; with or without subsidy it calls for a drastic restructuring of pricing practices, with opportunities for very substantial improvements in efficiency at critical points.

Exam Probability: **Low**

49. *Answer choices:*

(see index for correct answer)

- a. Production function
- b. Oligopsony
- c. Marginal cost
- d. Club good

Guidance: level 1

:: Macroeconomics and monetary economics ::

In economics, _____ is a decrease in the general price level of goods and services. _____ occurs when the inflation rate falls below 0% . Inflation reduces the value of currency over time, but _____ increases it. This allows more goods and services to be bought than before with the same amount of currency. _____ is distinct from disinflation, a slow-down in the inflation rate, i.e. when inflation declines to a lower rate but is still positive.

Exam Probability: **High**

50. *Answer choices:*

(see index for correct answer)

- a. Modern Monetary Theory
- b. Monetary inflation
- c. Absorption
- d. Debt Intolerance

Guidance: level 1

:: Taxation ::

A _____ is a tax incentive which allows certain taxpayers to subtract the amount of the credit they have accrued from the total they owe the state. It may also be a credit granted in recognition of taxes already paid or, as in the United Kingdom, a form of state support.

51. *Answer choices:*

(see index for correct answer)

- a. Tycoon Tax
- b. Seigniorage
- c. Tax Freedom Day
- d. subsidy

Guidance: level 1

:: Macroeconomic aggregates ::

In macroeconomics, _____ or Domestic Final Demand is the total demand for final goods and services in an economy at a given time. It is often called effective demand, though at other times this term is distinguished. This is the demand for the gross domestic product of a country. It specifies the amounts of goods and services that will be purchased at all possible price levels.

Exam Probability: **Low**

52. *Answer choices:*

(see index for correct answer)

- a. Aggregate expenditure
- b. Aggregate behavior

- c. aggregate supply

Guidance: level 1

:: Production economics ::

In microeconomics, _____ are the cost advantages that enterprises obtain due to their scale of operation , with cost per unit of output decreasing with increasing scale.

Exam Probability: **Low**

53. *Answer choices:*

(see index for correct answer)

- a. Constant elasticity of transformation
- b. Capacity utilization
- c. Indirect cost
- d. Diminishing marginal return

Guidance: level 1

:: Intertemporal economics ::

_____ is income not spent, or deferred consumption. Methods of _____ include putting money aside in, for example, a deposit account, a pension account, an investment fund, or as cash. _____ also involves reducing expenditures, such as recurring costs. In terms of personal finance, _____ generally specifies low-risk preservation of money, as in a deposit account, versus investment, wherein risk is a lot higher; in economics more broadly, it refers to any income not used for immediate consumption.

Exam Probability: **Low**

54. *Answer choices:*

(see index for correct answer)

- a. Intertemporal equilibrium
- b. Saving
- c. Time value of money
- d. Temporal discounting

Guidance: level 1

:: Protectionism ::

_____ is the economic policy of restricting imports from other countries through methods such as tariffs on imported goods, import quotas, and a variety of other government regulations. Proponents claim that protectionist policies shield the producers, businesses, and workers of the import-competing sector in the country from foreign competitors. However, they also reduce trade and adversely affect consumers in general , and harm the producers and workers in export sectors, both in the country implementing protectionist policies, and in the countries protected against.

Exam Probability: **Low**

55. *Answer choices:*

(see index for correct answer)

- a. Intrusionism
- b. Protectionism
- c. Importation Act 1463
- d. Neo-protectionism

Guidance: level 1

:: Capitalist systems ::

_____ is an economic system based on the private ownership of the means of production and their operation for profit. Characteristics central to _____ include private property, capital accumulation, wage labor, voluntary exchange, a price system, and competitive markets. In a capitalist market economy, decision-making and investment are determined by every owner of wealth, property or production ability in financial and capital markets, whereas prices and the distribution of goods and services are mainly determined by competition in goods and services markets.

Exam Probability: **Medium**

56. *Answer choices:*

(see index for correct answer)

- a. Capitalism
- b. Advanced capitalism
- c. New economy
- d. Coordinated market economy

Guidance: level 1

:: Employment compensation ::

_____ s are wages adjusted for inflation, or, equivalently, wages in terms of the amount of goods and services that can be bought. This term is used in contrast to nominal wages or unadjusted wages.

Exam Probability: **Low**

57. *Answer choices:*

(see index for correct answer)

- a. Idiosyncratic deals
- b. Annual leave
- c. Real wage
- d. Family wage

Guidance: level 1

:: Monetary policy ::

In monetary economics, a _____ is one of various closely related ratios of commercial bank money to central bank money under a fractional-reserve banking system. In one version it measures the maximum amount of commercial bank money that can be created, given a certain amount of central bank money and ignoring leakages into currency held by the non-bank public. That is, in a fractional-reserve banking system, the total amount of loans that commercial banks are allowed to extend when there are no leakages is equal to a multiple of the amount of reserves. This multiple is the reciprocal of the reserve ratio, and it is an economic multiplier. The actual ratio of money to central bank money, also called the _____ , is lower because some funds are held by the non-bank public as currency and most banks hold excess reserves

Exam Probability: **Low**

58. *Answer choices:*

(see index for correct answer)

- a. Money multiplier
- b. Excess reserves
- c. inflationary
- d. Shadow Open Market Committee

Guidance: level 1

:: International taxation ::

A _____ is a tax on imports or exports between sovereign states. It is a form of regulation of foreign trade and a policy that taxes foreign products to encourage or safeguard domestic industry. _____ s are the simplest and oldest instrument of trade policy. Traditionally, states have used them as a source of income. Now, they are among the most widely used instruments of protection, along with import and export quotas.

Exam Probability: **Medium**

59. *Answer choices:*

(see index for correct answer)

- a. Tax equalization
- b. Transactional net margin method
- c. Advance pricing agreement
- d. Tariff

Guidance: level 1

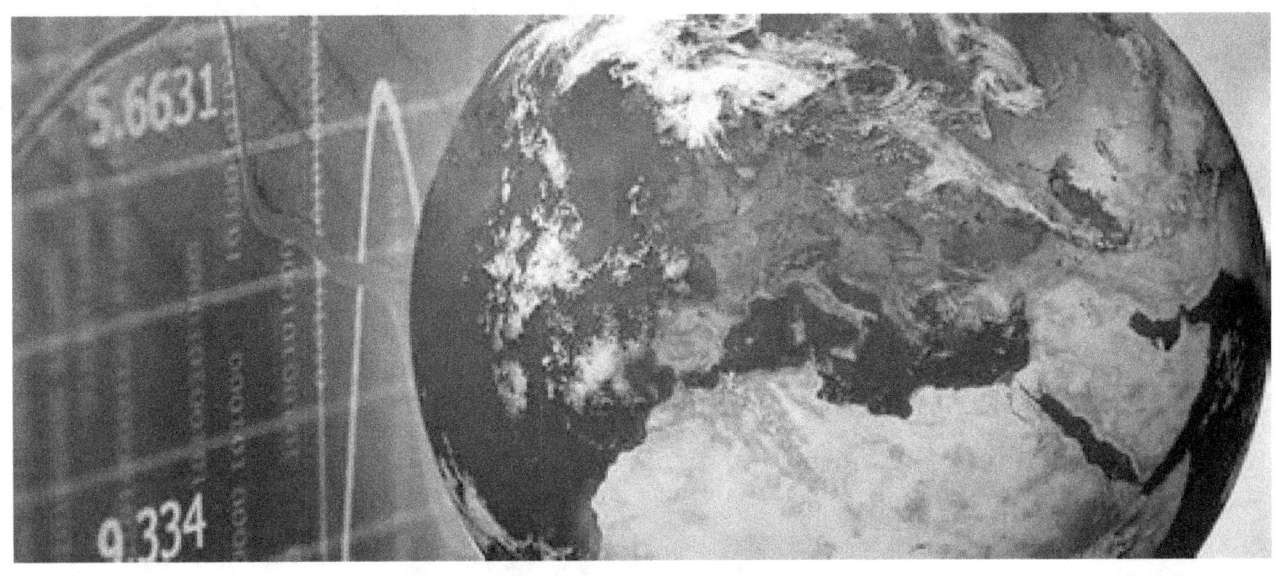

Fundamental economics

Economic analysis can be applied throughout society, in business, finance, health care, and government. Economic analysis is sometimes also applied to such diverse subjects as crime, education, the family, law, politics, religion, social institutions, war, science, and the environment.

:: Keynesian economics ::

_____ are a group of various macroeconomic theories about how in the short run – and especially during recessions – economic output is strongly influenced by aggregate demand . In the Keynesian view, named for British economist John Maynard Keynes, aggregate demand does not necessarily equal the productive capacity of the economy; instead, it is influenced by a host of factors and sometimes behaves erratically, affecting production, employment, and inflation.

Exam Probability: **High**

1. *Answer choices:*

(see index for correct answer)

- a. Hydraulic macroeconomics
- b. Underemployment equilibrium
- c. Paradox of toil
- d. Animal Spirits: How Human Psychology Drives the Economy, and Why It Matters for Global Capitalism

Guidance: level 1

:: Promotion and marketing communications ::

_____ is a marketing communication that employs an openly sponsored, non-personal message to promote or sell a product, service or idea. Sponsors of _____ are typically businesses wishing to promote their products or services. _____ is differentiated from public relations in that an advertiser pays for and has control over the message. It differs from personal selling in that the message is non-personal, i.e., not directed to a particular individual. _____ is communicated through various mass media, including traditional media such as newspapers, magazines, television, radio, outdoor _____ or direct mail; and new media such as search results, blogs, social media, websites or text messages. The actual presentation of the message in a medium is referred to as an advertisement, or "ad" or advert for short.

Exam Probability: **Medium**

2. *Answer choices:*

(see index for correct answer)

- a. One sheet
- b. Flat Eric
- c. Advertising
- d. Worthy Book

Guidance: level 1

:: Mathematical and quantitative methods (economics) ::

_____ is the study of mathematical models of strategic interaction between rational decision-makers. It has applications in all fields of social science, as well as in logic and computer science. Originally, it addressed zero-sum games, in which one person's gains result in losses for the other participants. Today, _____ applies to a wide range of behavioral relations, and is now an umbrella term for the science of logical decision making in humans, animals, and computers.

Exam Probability: **Low**

3. *Answer choices:*

(see index for correct answer)

- a. Kakutani fixed-point theorem
- b. Statistics
- c. Game theory
- d. Lagrangian

Guidance: level 1

:: Price indices ::

A _____ measures changes in the price level of market basket of consumer goods and services purchased by households.

Exam Probability: **Medium**

4. *Answer choices:*

(see index for correct answer)

- a. Christmas Price Index
- b. Prices received index
- c. Lipstick index
- d. Monetary Union Index of Consumer Prices

Guidance: level 1

:: Monetary policy ::

_____ is the process by which the monetary authority of a country, typically the central bank or currency board, controls either the cost of very short-term borrowing or the money supply, often targeting inflation rate or interest rate to ensure price stability and general trust in the currency.

Exam Probability: **Low**

5. *Answer choices:*

(see index for correct answer)

- a. market monetarist
- b. currency depreciation
- c. Monetary policy
- d. Money multiplier

Guidance: level 1

:: National accounts ::

_____ is a monetary measure of the market value of all the final goods and services produced in a period of time, often annually. GDP per capita does not, however, reflect differences in the cost of living and the inflation rates of the countries; therefore using a basis of GDP per capita at purchasing power parity is arguably more useful when comparing differences in living standards between nations.

Exam Probability: **Low**

6. *Answer choices:*

(see index for correct answer)

- a. Gross output
- b. nominal GDP
- c. Operating surplus
- d. Consumption of fixed capital

:: Monetary economics ::

The general _____ is a hypothetical daily measure of overall prices for some set of goods and services , in an economy or monetary union during a given interval , normalized relative to some base set. Typically, the general _____ is approximated with a daily price index, normally the Daily CPI. The general _____ can change more than once per day during hyperinflation.

Exam Probability: **High**

7. *Answer choices:*

(see index for correct answer)

- a. Financial rand
- b. Price level
- c. vault Cash
- d. Friedman rule

:: Asymmetric information ::

In economics, _____ occurs when someone increases their exposure to risk when insured, especially when a person takes more risks because someone else bears the cost of those risks. A _____ may occur where the actions of one party may change to the detriment of another after a financial transaction has taken place.

Exam Probability: **Low**

8. *Answer choices:*

(see index for correct answer)

- a. Screening
- b. The Market for Lemons
- c. Adverse selection
- d. Moral hazard

Guidance: level 1

:: Microeconomics ::

In financial accounting, an _____ is any resource owned by the business. Anything tangible or intangible that can be owned or controlled to produce value and that is held by a company to produce positive economic value is an _____ . Simply stated, _____ s represent value of ownership that can be converted into cash . The balance sheet of a firm records the monetary value of the _____ s owned by that firm. It covers money and other valuables belonging to an individual or to a business.

9. *Answer choices:*

(see index for correct answer)

- a. Economic shortage
- b. Incentive
- c. Substitution effect
- d. Asset

Guidance: level 1

:: Rationing and licensing ::

_____ is the controlled distribution of scarce resources, goods, services, or an artificial restriction of demand. _____ controls the size of the ration, which is one's allowed portion of the resources being distributed on a particular day or at a particular time. There are many forms of _____ , and in western civilization people experience some of them in daily life without realizing it.

Exam Probability: **Medium**

10. *Answer choices:*

(see index for correct answer)

- a. Outdoor water-use restriction
- b. Ration stamp

- c. Rationing
- d. Credit rationing

Guidance: level 1

:: Evaluation ::

_____ solving consists of using generic or ad hoc methods in an orderly manner to find solutions to _____ s. Some of the _____ -solving techniques developed and used in philosophy, artificial intelligence, computer science, engineering, mathematics, or medicine are related to mental _____ -solving techniques studied in psychology.

Exam Probability: **Medium**

11. *Answer choices:*

(see index for correct answer)

- a. Problem
- b. Ernest R. House
- c. Common Criteria
- d. Expression

Guidance: level 1

:: Macroeconomic aggregates ::

In macroeconomics, _____ or Domestic Final Demand is the total demand for final goods and services in an economy at a given time. It is often called effective demand, though at other times this term is distinguished. This is the demand for the gross domestic product of a country. It specifies the amounts of goods and services that will be purchased at all possible price levels.

Exam Probability: **Medium**

12. *Answer choices:*

(see index for correct answer)

- a. Aggregate expenditure
- b. aggregate supply
- c. Aggregate demand

Guidance: level 1

:: History of mining ::

_____ is the extraction of valuable minerals or other geological materials from the earth, usually from an ore body, lode, vein, seam, reef or placer deposit. These deposits form a mineralized package that is of economic interest to the miner.

Exam Probability: **High**

13. *Answer choices:*

(see index for correct answer)

- a. Western Mining Corporation
- b. Diodorus Siculus
- c. Bergregal
- d. Coal breaker

Guidance: level 1

:: Corporate finance ::

_____ or stock market launch is a type of public offering in which shares of a company are sold to institutional investors and usually also retail investors; an IPO is underwritten by one or more investment banks, who also arrange for the shares to be listed on one or more stock exchanges. Through this process, colloquially known as floating, or going public, a privately held company is transformed into a public company. _____ s can be used: to raise new equity capital for the company concerned; to monetize the investments of private shareholders such as company founders or private equity investors; and to enable easy trading of existing holdings or future capital raising by becoming publicly traded enterprises.

Exam Probability: **Medium**

14. *Answer choices:*

(see index for correct answer)

- a. Initial public offering
- b. Capital structure

- c. Conditional budgeting
- d. Takeover

Guidance: level 1

:: Microeconomics ::

_____ is a branch of economics that studies the behaviour of individuals and firms in making decisions regarding the allocation of scarce resources and the interactions among these individuals and firms.

Exam Probability: **Low**

15. *Answer choices:*

(see index for correct answer)

- a. Loyalty program
- b. Microeconomics
- c. Marginal cost
- d. Conjectural variation

Guidance: level 1

:: Financial markets ::

_____ or OMV is the price at which an asset would trade in a competitive auction setting. _____ is often used interchangeably with open _____ , fair value or fair _____ , although these terms have distinct definitions in different standards, and may or may not differ in some circumstances.

Exam Probability: **High**

16. *Answer choices:*

(see index for correct answer)

- a. Market value
- b. Special memorandum account
- c. Overnight market
- d. Market Identifier Code

Guidance: level 1

:: Operations research ::

Some scenarios associate "this kind of planning" with learning "life skills". _____ s are necessary, or at least useful, in situations where individuals need to know what time they must be at a specific location to receive a specific service, and where people need to accomplish a set of goals within a set time period.

Exam Probability: **Low**

17. *Answer choices:*

(see index for correct answer)

- a. Canadian traveller problem
- b. Economic order quantity
- c. Schedule
- d. Dynamic programming

Guidance: level 1

:: International economics ::

In modern monetary policy, a _____ is an official lowering of the value of a country's currency within a fixed exchange rate system, by which the monetary authority formally sets a new fixed rate with respect to a foreign reference currency or currency basket. In contrast, a depreciation is a decrease in a currency's value due to market forces under a floating exchange rate, not government or central bank policy actions.

Exam Probability: **Medium**

18. *Answer choices:*

(see index for correct answer)

- a. Swan diagram
- b. Bimetallism
- c. Oligopolistic reaction
- d. Devaluation

:: Economics terminology ::

The law or principle of _____ holds that under free trade, an agent will produce more of and consume less of a good for which they have a _____ . _____ is the economic reality describing the work gains from trade for individuals, firms, or nations, which arise from differences in their factor endowments or technological progress. In an economic model, agents have a _____ over others in producing a particular good if they can produce that good at a lower relative opportunity cost or autarky price, i.e. at a lower relative marginal cost prior to trade. One shouldn't compare the monetary costs of production or even the resource costs of production. Instead, one must compare the opportunity costs of producing goods across countries.

Exam Probability: **High**

19. *Answer choices:*

(see index for correct answer)

- a. Total revenue
- b. Cyclical deficit
- c. Comparative advantage
- d. Valuation effects

:: Environmental economics ::

_____ is the process of people maintaining change in a balanced environment, in which the exploitation of resources, the direction of investments, the orientation of technological development and institutional change are all in harmony and enhance both current and future potential to meet human needs and aspirations. For many in the field, _____ is defined through the following interconnected domains or pillars: environment, economic and social, which according to Fritjof Capra is based on the principles of Systems Thinking. Sub-domains of sustainable development have been considered also: cultural, technological and political. While sustainable development may be the organizing principle for _____ for some, for others, the two terms are paradoxical . Sustainable development is the development that meets the needs of the present without compromising the ability of future generations to meet their own needs. Brundtland Report for the World Commission on Environment and Development introduced the term of sustainable development.

Exam Probability: **High**

20. *Answer choices:*
(see index for correct answer)

- a. Pigou Club
- b. Centre for Water Economics, Environment and Policy
- c. Green certificate
- d. Sustainability

Guidance: level 1

:: World government ::

The _____ is an intergovernmental organization that is concerned with the regulation of international trade between nations. The WTO officially commenced on 1 January 1995 under the Marrakesh Agreement, signed by 124 nations on 15 April 1994, replacing the General Agreement on Tariffs and Trade , which commenced in 1948. It is the largest international economic organization in the world.

Exam Probability: **Low**

21. *Answer choices:*

(see index for correct answer)

- a. Caput Mundi
- b. The Shape of Things to Come
- c. World Trade Organization
- d. New World Order

Guidance: level 1

:: Industrial organization ::

In economics, specifically general equilibrium theory, a perfect market is defined by several idealizing conditions, collectively called _____ . In theoretical models where conditions of _____ hold, it has been theoretically demonstrated that a market will reach an equilibrium in which the quantity supplied for every product or service, including labor, equals the quantity demanded at the current price. This equilibrium would be a Pareto optimum.

22. *Answer choices:*

(see index for correct answer)

- a. Countervailing power
- b. Path dependence
- c. Quaternary sector of the economy
- d. Perfect competition

Guidance: level 1

:: Anti-competitive behaviour ::

In theories of competition in economics, a barrier to entry, or an economic barrier to entry, is a fixed cost that must be incurred by a new entrant, regardless of production or sales activities, into a market that incumbents do not have or have not had to incur.

Exam Probability: **Medium**

23. *Answer choices:*

(see index for correct answer)

- a. Horizontal territorial allocation
- b. Third line forcing
- c. United States v. General Electric Co.

- d. Barriers to entry

Guidance: level 1

:: Costs ::

In economics, _____ s, indirect costs or overheads are business expenses that are not dependent on the level of goods or services produced by the business. They tend to be time-related, such as interest or rents being paid per month, and are often referred to as overhead costs. This is in contrast to variable costs, which are volume-related and unknown at the beginning of the accounting year. For a simple example, such as a bakery, the monthly rent for the baking facilities, and the monthly payments for the security system and basic phone line are _____ s, as they do not change according to how much bread the bakery produces and sells. On the other hand, the wage costs of the bakery are variable, as the bakery will have to hire more workers if the production of bread increases. Economists reckon _____ as a entry barrier for new entrepreneurs.

Exam Probability: **Low**

24. *Answer choices:*

(see index for correct answer)

- a. Joint cost
- b. Cost competitiveness of fuel sources
- c. Manufacturing cost
- d. Prospective costs

Guidance: level 1

:: Property law ::

_____ is a legal designation for the ownership of property by non-governmental legal entities. _____ is distinguishable from public property, which is owned by a state entity; and from collective property, which is owned by a group of non-governmental entities. _____ can be either personal property or capital goods. _____ is a legal concept defined and enforced by a country's political system.

Exam Probability: **Low**

25. *Answer choices:*

(see index for correct answer)

- a. Equitable conversion
- b. Forced heirship
- c. Dower
- d. Private property

Guidance: level 1

:: Interest rates ::

An _____ is the amount of interest due per period, as a proportion of the amount lent, deposited or borrowed . The total interest on an amount lent or borrowed depends on the principal sum, the _____ , the compounding frequency, and the length of time over which it is lent, deposited or borrowed.

Exam Probability: **Low**

26. *Answer choices:*

(see index for correct answer)

- a. Official cash rate
- b. Interest rate
- c. Rule of 78s
- d. Overnight rate

Guidance: level 1

:: Labor economics ::

_____ is a situation in which everyone who wants a job can have work hours they need on "fair wages". Because people switch jobs, _____ involves a positive stable rate of unemployment. An economy with _____ might still have underemployment where part-time workers cannot find jobs appropriate to their skill level. In macroeconomics, _____ is sometimes defined as the level of employment at which there is no cyclical or deficient-demand unemployment.

Exam Probability: **High**

27. *Answer choices:*

(see index for correct answer)

- a. The Theory of Wages
- b. Guest worker program
- c. Full employment
- d. Non-wage labour costs

Guidance: level 1

:: Income ::

_____ is the consumption and saving opportunity gained by an entity within a specified timeframe, which is generally expressed in monetary terms. For households and individuals, " _____ is the sum of all the wages, salaries, profits, interest payments, rents, and other forms of earnings received in a given period of time."

Exam Probability: **Medium**

28. *Answer choices:*

(see index for correct answer)

- a. Income bracket
- b. Income
- c. Stipend
- d. Passive income

:: Foreign direct investment ::

A _____ is an investment in the form of a controlling ownership in a business in one country by an entity based in another country. It is thus distinguished from a foreign portfolio investment by a notion of direct control.

Exam Probability: **Medium**

29. *Answer choices:*

(see index for correct answer)

- a. Foreign direct investment
- b. Foreign direct investment in Romania
- c. Trade and Investment Framework Agreement
- d. Offshore financial centre

:: Commerce ::

In trade, _____ is a system of exchange where participants in a transaction directly exchange goods or services for other goods or services without using a medium of exchange, such as money. Economists distinguish _____ from gift economies in many ways; _____ , for example, features immediate reciprocal exchange, not delayed in time. _____ usually takes place on a bilateral basis, but may be multilateral . In most developed countries, _____ usually only exists parallel to monetary systems to a very limited extent. Market actors use _____ as a replacement for money as the method of exchange in times of monetary crisis, such as when currency becomes unstable or simply unavailable for conducting commerce.

Exam Probability: **High**

30. *Answer choices:*

(see index for correct answer)

- a. Sell-side analyst
- b. Requisition
- c. Barter
- d. Purchase discount

Guidance: level 1

:: Public finance ::

_____ or expenditure includes all government consumption, investment, and transfer payments. In national income accounting the acquisition by governments of goods and services for current use, to directly satisfy the individual or collective needs of the community, is classed as government final consumption expenditure. Government acquisition of goods and services intended to create future benefits, such as infrastructure investment or research spending, is classed as government investment . These two types of _____ , on final consumption and on gross capital formation, together constitute one of the major components of gross domestic product.

Exam Probability: **Low**

31. *Answer choices:*

(see index for correct answer)

- a. Barnett formula
- b. Lump-sum tax
- c. Government spending
- d. Public expenditure

Guidance: level 1

:: Banking ::

A _____ is a financial institution that accepts deposits from the public and creates credit. Lending activities can be performed either directly or indirectly through capital markets. Due to their importance in the financial stability of a country, _____ s are highly regulated in most countries. Most nations have institutionalized a system known as fractional reserve _____ ing under which _____ s hold liquid assets equal to only a portion of their current liabilities. In addition to other regulations intended to ensure liquidity, _____ s are generally subject to minimum capital requirements based on an international set of capital standards, known as the Basel Accords.

Exam Probability: **Medium**

32. *Answer choices:*

(see index for correct answer)

- a. Daylight overdraft
- b. Bank
- c. Foreign currency account
- d. Gold key

Guidance: level 1

:: Goods ::

In most contexts, the concept of _____ denotes the conduct that should be preferred when posed with a choice between possible actions. _____ is generally considered to be the opposite of evil, and is of interest in the study of morality, ethics, religion and philosophy. The specific meaning and etymology of the term and its associated translations among ancient and contemporary languages show substantial variation in its inflection and meaning depending on circumstances of place, history, religious, or philosophical context.

Exam Probability: **High**

33. *Answer choices:*

(see index for correct answer)

- a. Durable good
- b. Good
- c. Common good
- d. Speciality goods

Guidance: level 1

:: Monetary policy ::

In banking, _____ are bank reserves in excess of a reserve requirement set by a central bank.

Exam Probability: **Low**

34. *Answer choices:*

(see index for correct answer)

- a. Excess reserves
- b. Liquidity adjustment facility
- c. Impossible trinity
- d. Lombard credit

Guidance: level 1

:: Debt ::

A _____ is a colloquial term for the provision of financial help to a corporation or country which otherwise would be on the brink of failure or bankruptcy.

Exam Probability: **High**

35. *Answer choices:*

(see index for correct answer)

- a. Arrears
- b. Perpetual subordinated debt
- c. Overtrading
- d. Teacher Loan Forgiveness

Guidance: level 1

:: Philosophy of science ::

A _____ is a contemplative and rational type of abstract or generalizing thinking, or the results of such thinking. Depending on the context, the results might, for example, include generalized explanations of how nature works. The word has its roots in ancient Greek, but in modern use it has taken on several related meanings.

Exam Probability: **High**

36. *Answer choices:*

(see index for correct answer)

- a. God of the gaps
- b. Wholeness and the Implicate Order
- c. Experience
- d. Pessimistic induction

Guidance: level 1

:: Statistical terminology ::

In statistics, a _____ is a value that allows data to be measured over time in terms of some base period, usually through a price index, in order to distinguish between changes in the money value of a gross national product that come from a change in prices, and changes from a change in physical output. It is the measure of the price level for some quantity. A _____ serves as a price index in which the effects of inflation are nulled. It is the difference between real and nominal GDP.

Exam Probability: **Low**

37. *Answer choices:*

(see index for correct answer)

- a. Test statistic
- b. Cause of death
- c. Chain linking
- d. Deflator

Guidance: level 1

:: Demographics ::

_____ are the demographic cohort following the Silent Generation and preceding Generation X. Though there may be a few different timelines said to represent the birth years of the Baby Boom generation, the U.S. Census Bureau and many experts agree that the Baby Boom generation spans 18 birth years from 1946 to 1964. This leaves room for demographers and researchers to define and label cohort subsets if the characteristics and experiences of the youngest or oldest members correlate with or span two generations. When the term "baby boomer" is used in a cultural context, it becomes more difficult to achieve a consensus among scholars, demographers and researchers as to the precise birth years from a cultural perspective.

Exam Probability: **Low**

38. *Answer choices:*

(see index for correct answer)

- a. Baby Boomers
- b. Burnt Generation
- c. Sex selection
- d. Intergenerationality

Guidance: level 1

:: Financial markets ::

As money became a commodity, the _____ became a component of the financial market for assets involved in short-term borrowing, lending, buying and selling with original maturities of one year or less. Trading in _____ s is done over the counter and is wholesale.

39. *Answer choices:*

(see index for correct answer)

- a. Market liquidity
- b. Financial services
- c. Fution
- d. Money market

Guidance: level 1

:: Dividends ::

A _____ is a payment made by a corporation to its shareholders, usually as a distribution of profits. When a corporation earns a profit or surplus, the corporation is able to re-invest the profit in the business and pay a proportion of the profit as a _____ to shareholders. Distribution to shareholders may be in cash or, if the corporation has a _____ reinvestment plan, the amount can be paid by the issue of further shares or share repurchase. When _____ s are paid, shareholders typically must pay income taxes, and the corporation does not receive a corporate income tax deduction for the _____ payments.

Exam Probability: **Low**

40. *Answer choices:*

(see index for correct answer)

- a. Eisner v. Macomber
- b. Special dividend
- c. Dividend cover
- d. Dividend distribution tax

Guidance: level 1

:: Stock market ::

_____ is freedom from, or resilience against, potential harm caused by others. Beneficiaries of _____ may be of persons and social groups, objects and institutions, ecosystems or any other entity or phenomenon vulnerable to unwanted change by its environment.

Exam Probability: **Low**

41. *Answer choices:*

(see index for correct answer)

- a. Barbell strategy
- b. Event-driven investing
- c. Electronic communication network
- d. Security

Guidance: level 1

:: Economics ::

_____ is a situation in which the economy or an economic system could not produce any more of one good without sacrificing production of another good and without improving the production technology. In other words, _____ occurs when a good or a service is produced at the lowest possible cost. In simple terms, the concept is illustrated on a production possibility frontier , where all points on the curve are points of _____ . An equilibrium may be productively efficient without being allocatively efficient i.e. it may result in a distribution of goods where social welfare is not maximized. It is one type of economic efficiency.

Exam Probability: **Low**

42. *Answer choices:*

(see index for correct answer)

- a. Productive efficiency
- b. Relational contract
- c. Market rate
- d. Restoration Economy

Guidance: level 1

:: Economic policy ::

_____ is a monetary policy regime in which a central bank has an explicit target inflation rate for the medium term and announces this inflation target to the public. The assumption is that the best that monetary policy can do to support long-term growth of the economy is to maintain price stability. The central bank uses interest rates, its main short-term monetary instrument.

43. *Answer choices:*

(see index for correct answer)

- a. Quantitative easing
- b. Demand management
- c. Inflation targeting
- d. Centre of Full Employment and Equity

Guidance: level 1

:: Classical economics ::

_____ or classical political economy is a school of thought in economics that flourished, primarily in Britain, in the late 18th and early-to-mid 19th century. Its main thinkers are held to be Adam Smith, Jean-Baptiste Say, David Ricardo, Thomas Robert Malthus, and John Stuart Mill. These economists produced a theory of market economies as largely self-regulating systems, governed by natural laws of production and exchange .

44. *Answer choices:*

(see index for correct answer)

- a. Classical economics
- b. Circulating capital
- c. Underconsumption
- d. Primitive accumulation of capital

Guidance: level 1

:: Federal Reserve Banks ::

A _____ is a regional bank of the Federal Reserve System, the central banking system of the United States. There are twelve in total, one for each of the twelve Federal Reserve Districts that were created by the Federal Reserve Act of 1913. The banks are jointly responsible for implementing the monetary policy set forth by the Federal Open Market Committee, and are divided as follows.

Exam Probability: **High**

45. *Answer choices:*

(see index for correct answer)

- a. Federal Reserve Bank of Atlanta
- b. Federal Reserve Bank of San Francisco, Los Angeles Branch
- c. Federal Reserve Bank
- d. Federal Reserve Bank of Chicago Detroit Branch Building

:: Business cycle ::

The _____ , also known as the economic cycle or trade cycle, is the downward and upward movement of gross domestic product around its long-term growth trend. The length of a _____ is the period of time containing a single boom and contraction in sequence. These fluctuations typically involve shifts over time between periods of relatively rapid economic growth and periods of relative stagnation or decline .

Exam Probability: **Low**

46. *Answer choices:*

(see index for correct answer)

- a. Soft landing
- b. Business cycle
- c. Economic recovery
- d. Reference date

:: Property ::

_____ , in the abstract, is what belongs to or with something, whether as an attribute or as a component of said thing. In the context of this article, it is one or more components , whether physical or incorporeal, of a person's estate; or so belonging to, as in being owned by, a person or jointly a group of people or a legal entity like a corporation or even a society. Depending on the nature of the _____ , an owner of _____ has the right to consume, alter, share, redefine, rent, mortgage, pawn, sell, exchange, transfer, give away or destroy it, or to exclude others from doing these things, as well as to perhaps abandon it; whereas regardless of the nature of the _____ , the owner thereof has the right to properly use it , or at the very least exclusively keep it.

Exam Probability: **High**

47. *Answer choices:*

(see index for correct answer)

- a. Croft
- b. Property rights
- c. Property
- d. Counter-mapping

Guidance: level 1

:: New Deal ::

The _____ was a series of programs, public work projects, financial reforms, and regulations enacted by President Franklin D. Roosevelt in the United States between 1933 and 1936. It responded to needs for relief, reform, and recovery from the Great Depression. Major federal programs included the Civilian Conservation Corps , the Civil Works Administration , the Farm Security Administration , the National Industrial Recovery Act of 1933 and the Social Security Administration . They provided support for farmers, the unemployed, youth and the elderly. The _____ included new constraints and safeguards on the banking industry and efforts to re-inflate the economy after prices had fallen sharply. _____ programs included both laws passed by Congress as well as presidential executive orders during the first term of the presidency of Franklin D. Roosevelt.

Exam Probability: **High**

48. *Answer choices:*

(see index for correct answer)

- a. Retirement, Survivors, Disability Insurance
- b. New Deal
- c. Conservative Manifesto
- d. New Deal coalition

Guidance: level 1

:: Accounting terminology ::

In financial accounting, a _____ or statement of financial position or statement of financial condition is a summary of the financial balances of an individual or organization, whether it be a sole proprietorship, a business partnership, a corporation, private limited company or other organization such as Government or not-for-profit entity. Assets, liabilities and ownership equity are listed as of a specific date, such as the end of its financial year. A _____ is often described as a "snapshot of a company's financial condition". Of the four basic financial statements, the _____ is the only statement which applies to a single point in time of a business' calendar year.

Exam Probability: **Low**

49. *Answer choices:*

(see index for correct answer)

- a. Capital expenditure
- b. Balance sheet
- c. Profit and loss statement
- d. Generally Accepted Privacy Principles

Guidance: level 1

:: Income distribution ::

In economics, _____ is how a nation's total GDP is distributed amongst its population. Income and its distribution have always been a central concern of economic theory and economic policy. Classical economists such as Adam Smith, Thomas Malthus, and David Ricardo were mainly concerned with factor _____ , that is, the distribution of income between the main factors of production, land, labour and capital. Modern economists have also addressed this issue, but have been more concerned with the distribution of income across individuals and households. Important theoretical and policy concerns include the balance between income inequality and economic growth, and their often inverse relationship.

Exam Probability: **Low**

50. *Answer choices:*

(see index for correct answer)

- a. Winner-Take-All Politics
- b. Income distribution
- c. The rich get richer and the poor get poorer
- d. Factor income

Guidance: level 1

:: Capital (economics) ::

_____ is any economic resource measured in terms of money used by entrepreneurs and businesses to buy what they need to make their products or to provide their services to the sector of the economy upon which their operation is based, i.e. retail, corporate, investment banking, etc.

51. *Answer choices:*

(see index for correct answer)

- a. Public capital
- b. Individual capital
- c. Cost of capital
- d. Patient capital

Guidance: level 1

:: Macroeconomic aggregates ::

In economics, _____ or Domestic Final Supply is the total supply of goods and services that firms in a national economy plan on selling during a specific time period. It is the total amount of goods and services that firms are willing and able to sell at a given price level in an economy.

Exam Probability: **Low**

52. *Answer choices:*

(see index for correct answer)

- a. Aggregate supply
- b. Aggregate demand
- c. Aggregate behavior

:: Microeconomics ::

In economics, _____ is the change in the total cost that arises when the quantity produced is incremented by one unit; that is, it is the cost of producing one more unit of a good. Intuitively, _____ at each level of production includes the cost of any additional inputs required to produce the next unit. At each level of production and time period being considered, _____ s include all costs that vary with the level of production, whereas other costs that do not vary with production are fixed and thus have no _____ . For example, the _____ of producing an automobile will generally include the costs of labor and parts needed for the additional automobile but not the fixed costs of the factory that have already been incurred. In practice, marginal analysis is segregated into short and long-run cases, so that, over the long run, all costs become marginal. Where there are economies of scale, prices set at _____ will fail to cover total costs, thus requiring a subsidy. _____ pricing is not a matter of merely lowering the general level of prices with the aid of a subsidy; with or without subsidy it calls for a drastic restructuring of pricing practices, with opportunities for very substantial improvements in efficiency at critical points.

Exam Probability: **Medium**

53. *Answer choices:*

(see index for correct answer)

- a. Ex-ante
- b. Preference
- c. Production function

- d. Marginal cost

Guidance: level 1

:: Economic policy ::

The _____ of governments covers the systems for setting levels of taxation, government budgets, the money supply and interest rates as well as the labour market, national ownership, and many other areas of government interventions into the economy.

Exam Probability: **Low**

54. *Answer choices:*

(see index for correct answer)

- a. Centre of Full Employment and Equity
- b. The Other Canon Foundation
- c. Economic policy
- d. Job guarantee

Guidance: level 1

:: Economics curves ::

In economics, the _____ is the graph depicting the relationship between the price of a certain commodity and the amount of it that consumers are willing and able to purchase at any given price. It is a graphic representation of a market demand schedule. The _____ for all consumers together follows from the _____ of every individual consumer: the individual demands at each price are added together, assuming independent decision-making.

55. *Answer choices:*

(see index for correct answer)

- a. Cost curve
- b. Great Gatsby curve
- c. Lorenz curve
- d. Kuznets curve

Guidance: level 1

:: Financial crises ::

In economics, _____ is very high and typically accelerating inflation. It quickly erodes the real value of the local currency, as the prices of all goods increase. This causes people to minimize their holdings in that currency as they usually switch to more stable foreign currencies, often the US Dollar. Prices typically remain stable in terms of other relatively stable currencies.

56. *Answer choices:*

(see index for correct answer)

- a. Kennedy Slide of 1962
- b. Hyperinflation
- c. Speculative attack
- d. Panic of 1893

Guidance: level 1

:: Economics terminology ::

In economics, a _____ is a person of legal employment age who is not actively seeking employment or who has not found employment after long-term unemployment, but who would prefer to be working. This is usually because an individual has given up looking, hence the term "discouraged".

Exam Probability: **Low**

57. *Answer choices:*

(see index for correct answer)

- a. Mechanism
- b. Low-level equilibrium trap
- c. Discouraged worker
- d. Dual-beta

:: Competition (economics) ::

_____ arises whenever at least two parties strive for a goal which cannot be shared: where one's gain is the other's loss .

Exam Probability: **Medium**

58. *Answer choices:*

(see index for correct answer)

- a. Blindspots analysis
- b. Competitor analysis
- c. Fuld-Gilad-Herring Academy of Competitive Intelligence
- d. Competition

:: Macroeconomics ::

_____ is a branch of economics dealing with the performance, structure, behavior, and decision-making of an economy as a whole. This includes regional, national, and global economies. Macroeconomists study aggregated indicators such as GDP, unemployment rates, national income, price indices, and the interrelations among the different sectors of the economy to better understand how the whole economy functions. They also develop models that explain the relationship between such factors as national income, output, consumption, unemployment, inflation, saving, investment, international trade, and international finance.

Exam Probability: **Low**

59. *Answer choices:*

(see index for correct answer)

- a. Boukaseff scale
- b. Macroeconomics
- c. Macroeconomic policy instruments
- d. Adaptive expectations

Guidance: level 1

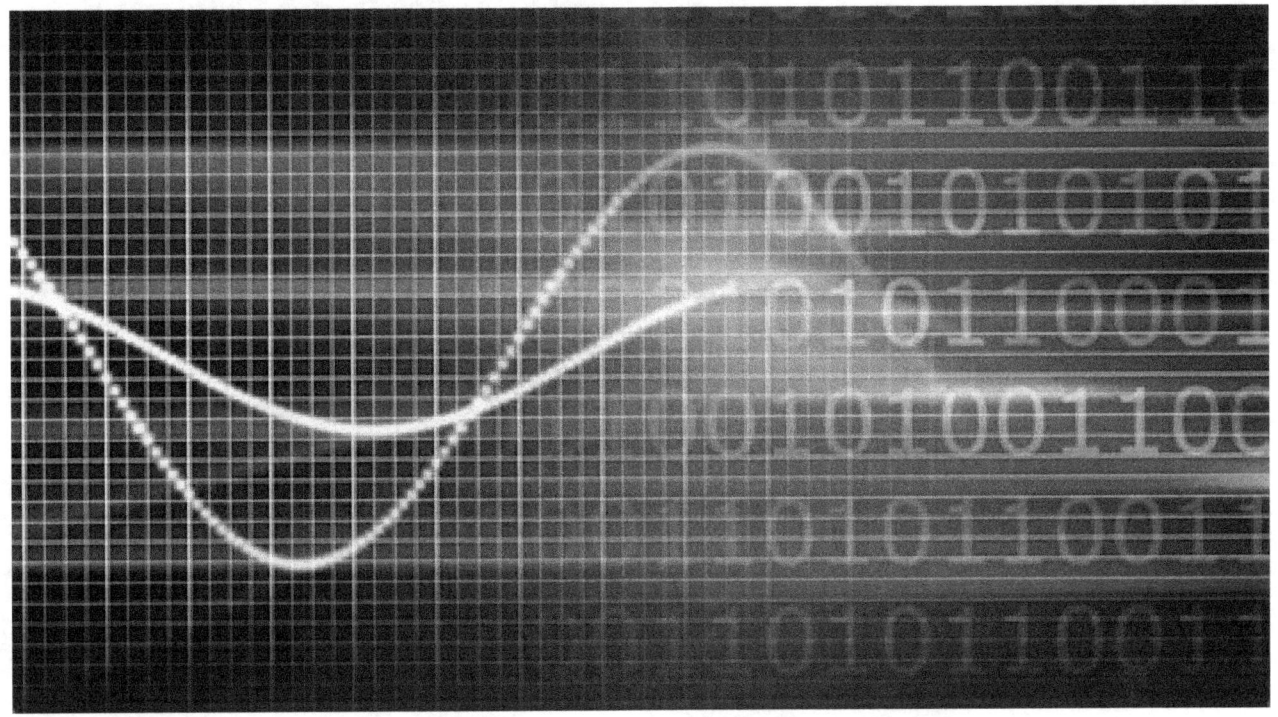

Mathematical and quantitative methods

Mathematical economics is the application of mathematical methods to represent theories and analyze problems in economics. By convention, these applied methods are beyond simple geometry, such as differential and integral calculus, difference and differential equations, matrix algebra, mathematical programming, and other computational methods.

:: Algebra ::

In linear algebra, the _____ is a scalar value that can be computed from the elements of a square matrix and encodes certain properties of the linear transformation described by the matrix. The _____ of a matrix A is denoted det, det A, or A. Geometrically, it can be viewed as the volume scaling factor of the linear transformation described by the matrix. This is also the signed volume of the n-dimensional parallelepiped spanned by the column or row vectors of the matrix. The _____ is positive or negative according to whether the linear mapping preserves or reverses the orientation of n-space.

Exam Probability: **Medium**

1. *Answer choices:*

(see index for correct answer)

- a. monomial
- b. polynomial

Guidance: level 1

:: Statistical charts and diagrams ::

A _____ is a diagram that shows all possible logical relations between a finite collection of different sets. These diagrams depict elements as points in the plane, and sets as regions inside closed curves. A _____ consists of multiple overlapping closed curves, usually circles, each representing a set. The points inside a curve labelled S represent elements of the set S, while points outside the boundary represent elements not in the set S. This lends to easily read visualizations; for example, the set of all elements that are members of both sets S and T, S n T, is represented visually by the area of overlap of the regions S and T. In _____ s the curves are overlapped in every possible way, showing all possible relations between the sets. They are thus a special case of Euler diagrams, which do not necessarily show all relations. _____ s were conceived around 1880 by John Venn. They are used to teach elementary set theory, as well as illustrate simple set relationships in probability, logic, statistics, linguistics, and computer science.

Exam Probability: **Medium**

2. *Answer choices:*

(see index for correct answer)

- a. Defect concentration diagram
- b. Temporal Raster Plot
- c. Venn diagram
- d. Volcano plot

Guidance: level 1

:: Validity (statistics) ::

_____ is the extent to which a test is subjectively viewed as covering the concept it purports to measure. It refers to the transparency or relevance of a test as it appears to test participants. In other words, a test can be said to have _____ if it "looks like" it is going to measure what it is supposed to measure. For instance, if a test is prepared to measure whether students can perform multiplication, and the people to whom it is shown all agree that it looks like a good test of multiplication ability, this demonstrates _____ of the test. _____ is often contrasted with content validity and construct validity.

Exam Probability: **High**

3. *Answer choices:*

(see index for correct answer)

- a. Verification and validation
- b. Nomological network
- c. Concurrent validity
- d. Face validity

Guidance: level 1

:: Analysis of variance ::

In statistics, the _____ is an extension of the one-way ANOVA that examines the influence of two different categorical independent variables on one continuous dependent variable. The two-way ANOVA not only aims at assessing the main effect of each independent variable but also if there is any interaction between them.

4. *Answer choices:*

(see index for correct answer)

- a. Main effect
- b. Standardized mean of a contrast variable
- c. Two-way analysis of variance
- d. random effect

Guidance: level 1

:: Probability distributions ::

In probability theory and statistics, a _____ is a mathematical function that provides the probabilities of occurrence of different possible outcomes in an experiment. In more technical terms, the _____ is a description of a random phenomenon in terms of the probabilities of events. For instance, if the random variable X is used to denote the outcome of a coin toss , then the _____ of X would take the value 0.5 for X = heads, and 0.5 for X = tails . Examples of random phenomena can include the results of an experiment or survey.

5. *Answer choices:*

(see index for correct answer)

- a. Xenakis distribution
- b. Generalized gamma distribution
- c. Probability distribution
- d. Weibull distribution

Guidance: level 1

:: Types of functions ::

In mathematics, an _____ function or injection or one-to-one function is a function that preserves distinctness: it never maps distinct elements of its domain to the same element of its codomain. In other words, every element of the function's codomain is the image of at most one element of its domain. The term one-to-one function must not be confused with one-to-one correspondence , which uniquely maps all elements in both domain and codomain to each other .

Exam Probability: **Low**

6. *Answer choices:*
(see index for correct answer)

- a. Constant function
- b. even function
- c. Discontinuous function
- d. weighted

Guidance: level 1

:: Risk analysis ::

_____ is the identification, evaluation, and prioritization of risks followed by coordinated and economical application of resources to minimize, monitor, and control the probability or impact of unfortunate events or to maximize the realization of opportunities.

Exam Probability: **Low**

7. *Answer choices:*

(see index for correct answer)

- a. Supply chain risk management
- b. Event tree
- c. Risk management
- d. Criticality index

Guidance: level 1

:: Consumer theory ::

In microeconomics, a consumer's _____ correspondence is the demand of a consumer over a bundle of goods that minimizes their expenditure while delivering a fixed level of utility. If the correspondence is actually a function, it is referred to as the _____ function, or compensated demand function. The function is named after John Hicks.

8. *Answer choices:*

(see index for correct answer)

- a. Snob effect
- b. End-of-life
- c. Hicksian demand
- d. Marginal rate of substitution

Guidance: level 1

:: Time series models ::

In time series analysis, the _____ , also known as moving-average process, is a common approach for modeling univariate time series. The _____ specifies that the output variable depends linearly on the current and various past values of a stochastic term.

Exam Probability: **High**

9. *Answer choices:*

(see index for correct answer)

- a. Error correction model
- b. SETAR
- c. Moving-average model

- d. Distributed lag

Guidance: level 1

:: Regression analysis ::

In statistical data analysis the _____ is a quantity that appears as part of a standard way of presenting results of such analyses. It is defined as being the sum, over all observations, of the squared differences of each observation from the overall mean.

Exam Probability: **Medium**

10. *Answer choices:*
(see index for correct answer)

- a. Nonparametric regression
- b. Regression model validation
- c. Bayesian multivariate linear regression
- d. Total sum of squares

Guidance: level 1

:: Summary statistics ::

_____ is the number of occurrences of a repeating event per unit of time. It is also referred to as temporal _____ , which emphasizes the contrast to spatial _____ and angular _____ . The period is the duration of time of one cycle in a repeating event, so the period is the reciprocal of the _____ . For example: if a newborn baby's heart beats at a _____ of 120 times a minute, its period—the time interval between beats—is half a second . _____ is an important parameter used in science and engineering to specify the rate of oscillatory and vibratory phenomena, such as mechanical vibrations, audio signals , radio waves, and light.

Exam Probability: **High**

11. *Answer choices:*

(see index for correct answer)

- a. Mean percentage error
- b. Quartile
- c. Nonparametric skew
- d. Quantile

Guidance: level 1

:: Causal inference ::

_____ is the validity of applying the conclusions of a scientific study outside the context of that study. In other words, it is the extent to which the results of a study can be generalized to and across other situations, people, stimuli, and times. In contrast, internal validity is the validity of conclusions drawn within the context of a particular study. Because general conclusions are almost always a goal in research, _____ is an important property of any study. Mathematical analysis of _____ concerns a determination of whether generalization across heterogeneous populations is feasible, and devising statistical and computational methods that produce valid generalizations.

Exam Probability: **High**

12. *Answer choices:*

(see index for correct answer)

- a. Probabilistic causation
- b. Internal validity
- c. Simpson's Paradox
- d. Covariation model

Guidance: level 1

:: Statistical tests ::

A _____ is any statistical test for which the distribution of the test statistic under the null hypothesis can be approximated by a normal distribution. Because of the central limit theorem, many test statistics are approximately normally distributed for large samples. For each significance level, the _____ has a single critical value which makes it more convenient than the Student's t-test which has separate critical values for each sample size. Therefore, many statistical tests can be conveniently performed as approximate _____ s if the sample size is large or the population variance is known. If the population variance is unknown and the sample size is not large , the Student's t-test may be more appropriate.

Exam Probability: **Medium**

13. *Answer choices:*

(see index for correct answer)

- a. Spearman's rho
- b. Sequential probability ratio test
- c. Spearman's rank correlation coefficient
- d. ABX test

Guidance: level 1

:: Data analysis ::

In statistics, the _____ is a measure that is used to quantify the amount of variation or dispersion of a set of data values. A low _____ indicates that the data points tend to be close to the mean of the set, while a high _____ indicates that the data points are spread out over a wider range of values.

Exam Probability: **Medium**

14. *Answer choices:*

(see index for correct answer)

- a. Lincoln index
- b. Data reduction
- c. Standard deviation
- d. TinkerPlots

Guidance: level 1

:: Time series analysis ::

A _____ is a type of statistical hypothesis test in which the null hypothesis is well specified, but the alternative hypothesis is more loosely specified. Tests constructed in this context can have the property of being at least moderately powerful against a wide range of departures from the null hypothesis. Thus, in applied statistics, a _____ provides a reasonable way of proceeding as a general check of a model's match to a dataset where there are many different ways in which the model may depart from the underlying data generating process. Use of such tests avoids having to be very specific about the particular type of departure being tested.

15. *Answer choices:*

(see index for correct answer)

- a. Autocorrelation technique
- b. Phase dispersion minimization
- c. Unit root test
- d. Portmanteau test

Guidance: level 1

:: Economics terminology ::

In economics, a _____ or reference period is a point in time used as a reference point for comparison with other periods. It is generally used as a benchmark for measuring financial or economic data. _____ s typically provide a point of reference for economic studies, consumer demand, and unemployment benefit claims.

Exam Probability: **High**

16. *Answer choices:*

(see index for correct answer)

- a. Electronic payment advice
- b. Market cannibalism

- c. Marginal value
- d. Base period

Guidance: level 1

:: Statistical models ::

A _____ is a type of mathematical model that is applied to the study of population dynamics.

Exam Probability: **Low**

17. *Answer choices:*

(see index for correct answer)

- a. Exponential dispersion model
- b. Mixture model
- c. Discriminative model
- d. Predictive modelling

Guidance: level 1

:: Mathematical finance ::

In economics, an _____ is the inverse function of a demand function. The _____ views price as a function of quantity.

Exam Probability: **Low**

18. *Answer choices:*

(see index for correct answer)

- a. Convexity
- b. Business mathematics
- c. Accumulation function
- d. Financial correlation

Guidance: level 1

:: Seasonality ::

_____ is a statistical method for removing the seasonal component of a time series that exhibits a seasonal pattern. It is usually done when wanting to analyse the trend, and cyclical deviations from trend, of a time series independently of the seasonal components. It is normal to report seasonally adjusted data for unemployment rates to reveal the underlying trends and cycles in labor markets. Many economic phenomena have seasonal cycles, such as agricultural production and consumer consumption, e.g. greater consumption leading up to Christmas. It is necessary to adjust for this component in order to understand what underlying trends are in the economy and so official statistics are often adjusted to remove seasonal components.

19. *Answer choices:*

(see index for correct answer)

- a. Season of birth
- b. Seasonality
- c. Seasonally adjusted annual rate
- d. Seasonal adjustment

Guidance: level 1

:: Statistical theory ::

In statistics, a _____ or finite-sample distribution is the probability distribution of a given random-sample-based statistic. If an arbitrarily large number of samples, each involving multiple observations , were separately used in order to compute one value of a statistic for each sample, then the _____ is the probability distribution of the values that the statistic takes on. In many contexts, only one sample is observed, but the _____ can be found theoretically.

20. *Answer choices:*

(see index for correct answer)

- a. Statistical theory

- b. Sampling distribution
- c. A priori probability
- d. Decoupling

Guidance: level 1

:: Knowledge representation ::

_____ is "data [information] that provides information about other data". Many distinct types of _____ exist, among these descriptive _____ , structural _____ , administrative _____ , reference _____ and statistical _____ .

Exam Probability: **High**

21. *Answer choices:*
(see index for correct answer)

- a. Metadata
- b. FrameNet
- c. Closed world assumption
- d. Yale shooting problem

Guidance: level 1

:: Mathematical economics ::

A _____ is commonly referred to as a monetary value assigned to currently unknowable or difficult-to-calculate costs. It is based on the willingness to pay principle - in the absence of market prices, the most accurate measure of the value of a good or service is what people are willing to give up in order to get it. Shadow pricing is often calculated on certain assumptions and premises. As a result, it is subjective and somewhat imprecise and inaccurate. The origin of these costs is typically due to an externalization of costs or an unwillingness to recalculate a system to account for marginal production. For example, consider a firm that already has a factory full of equipment and staff. They might estimate the _____ for a few more units of production as simply the cost of the overtime. In this manner, some goods and services have near zero _____ s, for example information goods. Less formally, a _____ can be thought of as the cost of decisions made at the margin without consideration for the total cost.

Exam Probability: **Low**

22. *Answer choices:*

(see index for correct answer)

- a. Isoelastic function
- b. Uncertainty modeling
- c. Elasticity of a function
- d. Wicksellian Differential

Guidance: level 1

:: Financial risk ::

The _____ on a financial investment is the expected value of its return . It is a measure of the center of the distribution of the random variable that is the return.

Exam Probability: **High**

23. *Answer choices:*

(see index for correct answer)

- a. ORRF Risk Research Forum
- b. RiskMetrics
- c. Model risk
- d. Expected return

Guidance: level 1

:: Multivariate statistics ::

In statistics, a _____ is a central or typical value for a probability distribution. It may also be called a center or location of the distribution. Colloquially, measures of _____ are often called averages. The term _____ dates from the late 1920s.

Exam Probability: **Medium**

24. *Answer choices:*

(see index for correct answer)

- a. Dimensionality reduction
- b. Data matrix
- c. Central tendency
- d. Multivariate random variable

Guidance: level 1

:: Statistical charts and diagrams ::

A _____ is a type of plot or mathematical diagram using Cartesian coordinates to display values for typically two variables for a set of data. If the points are coded , one additional variable can be displayed. The data are displayed as a collection of points, each having the value of one variable determining the position on the horizontal axis and the value of the other variable determining the position on the vertical axis.

Exam Probability: **Low**

25. *Answer choices:*
(see index for correct answer)

- a. Double mass analysis
- b. Temporal Raster Plot
- c. Scatter plot
- d. P-chart

Guidance: level 1

:: Economics ::

_____ is the process in which a nation is being improved in the sector of the economic, political, and social well-being of its people. The term has been used frequently by economists, politicians, and others in the 20th and 21st centuries. The concept, however, has been in existence in the West for centuries. "Modernization, "westernization", and especially "industrialization" are other terms often used while discussing _____ . _____ has a direct relationship with the environment and environmental issues. _____ is very often confused with industrial development, even in some academic sources.

Exam Probability: **High**

26. *Answer choices:*

(see index for correct answer)

- a. Hedonimetry
- b. Economic development
- c. Lean consumption
- d. Hard asset

Guidance: level 1

:: Exchange algorithms ::

In linear algebra, _____ is an algorithm for solving systems of linear equations. It is usually understood as a sequence of operations performed on the corresponding matrix of coefficients. This method can also be used to find the rank of a matrix, to calculate the determinant of a matrix, and to calculate the inverse of an invertible square matrix. The method is named after Carl Friedrich Gauss , although it was known to Chinese mathematicians as early as 179 A.D. .

Exam Probability: **Low**

27. *Answer choices:*

(see index for correct answer)

- a. Pivot element
- b. Gaussian elimination

Guidance: level 1

:: Statistical inference ::

In statistics, _____ is the use of sample data to calculate an interval of plausible values of an unknown population parameter; this is in contrast to point estimation, which gives a single value. Jerzy Neyman identified _____ as distinct from point estimation . In doing so, he recognized that then-recent work quoting results in the form of an estimate plus-or-minus a standard deviation indicated that _____ was actually the problem statisticians really had in mind.

Exam Probability: **High**

28. *Answer choices:*

(see index for correct answer)

- a. Formal epistemology
- b. Transferable belief model
- c. Uncomfortable science
- d. Interval estimation

Guidance: level 1

:: Statistical ratios ::

In statistics, the _____ is the difference between the largest and smallest data in a sample measured in units of sample standard deviations.

Exam Probability: **High**

29. *Answer choices:*

(see index for correct answer)

- a. Studentized range
- b. Standardized mortality ratio
- c. Strikeout-to-walk ratio
- d. Response-rate ratio

Guidance: level 1

:: Statistical charts and diagrams ::

A _____ or stem-and-leaf plot is a device for presenting quantitative data in a graphical format, similar to a histogram, to assist in visualizing the shape of a distribution. They evolved from Arthur Bowl's work in the early 1900s, and are useful tools in exploratory data analysis. Stemplots became more commonly used in the 1980s after the publication of John Tukey's book on exploratory data analysis in 1977. The popularity during those years is attributable to their use of monospaced typestyles that allowed computer technology of the time to easily produce the graphics. Modern computers' superior graphic capabilities have meant these techniques are less often used.

Exam Probability: **Low**

30. *Answer choices:*

(see index for correct answer)

- a. Stem-and-leaf display
- b. Cumulative flow diagram
- c. Rank abundance curve
- d. Chernoff face

Guidance: level 1

:: Statistical software ::

_____ is a statistics package developed at the Pennsylvania State University by researchers Barbara F. Ryan, Thomas A. Ryan, Jr., and Brian L. Joiner in 1972. It began as a light version of OMNITAB 80, a statistical analysis program by NIST. Statistical analysis software such as _____ automates calculations and the creation of graphs, allowing the user to focus more on the analysis of data and the interpretation of results. It is compatible with other _____ , Inc. software.

Exam Probability: **Medium**

31. *Answer choices:*

(see index for correct answer)

- a. Epi Info
- b. Statgraphics
- c. ASReml
- d. Minitab

Guidance: level 1

:: Statistical charts and diagrams ::

A _____ is a circular statistical graphic, which is divided into slices to illustrate numerical proportion. In a _____ , the arc length of each slice , is proportional to the quantity it represents. While it is named for its resemblance to a pie which has been sliced, there are variations on the way it can be presented. The earliest known _____ is generally credited to William Playfair's Statistical Breviary of 1801.

32. *Answer choices:*

(see index for correct answer)

- a. Spaghetti plot
- b. Dual-flashlight plot
- c. P-chart
- d. Pie chart

Guidance: level 1

:: Causal inference ::

_____ is the extent to which a piece of evidence supports a claim about cause and effect, within the context of a particular study. It is one of the most important properties of scientific studies, and is an important concept in reasoning about evidence more generally. _____ is determined by how well a study can rule out alternative explanations for its findings . It contrasts with external validity, the extent to which results can justify conclusions about other contexts .

Exam Probability: **High**

33. *Answer choices:*

(see index for correct answer)

- a. Internal validity

- b. Causality
- c. External validity
- d. Qualitative comparative analysis

Guidance: level 1

:: Time series analysis ::

_____ is a rule of thumb technique for smoothing time series data using the exponential window function. Whereas in the simple moving average the past observations are weighted equally, exponential functions are used to assign exponentially decreasing weights over time. It is an easily learned and easily applied procedure for making some determination based on prior assumptions by the user, such as seasonality. _____ is often used for analysis of time-series data.

Exam Probability: **High**

34. *Answer choices:*
(see index for correct answer)

- a. Long-range dependency
- b. Linear prediction
- c. Exponential smoothing
- d. Johansen test

Guidance: level 1

:: Statistical charts and diagrams ::

The _____ is a graphical technique to identify substantive departures from normality. This includes identifying outliers, skewness, kurtosis, a need for transformations, and mixtures. _____ s are made of raw data, residuals from model fits, and estimated parameters.

Exam Probability: **High**

35. *Answer choices:*

(see index for correct answer)

- a. Normal probability plot
- b. X-bar chart
- c. Defect concentration diagram
- d. Venn diagram

Guidance: level 1

:: Bayesian statistics ::

In Bayesian statistical inference, a _____ distribution, often simply called the prior, of an uncertain quantity is the probability distribution that would express one's beliefs about this quantity before some evidence is taken into account. For example, the prior could be the probability distribution representing the relative proportions of voters who will vote for a particular politician in a future election. The unknown quantity may be a parameter of the model or a latent variable rather than an observable variable.

Exam Probability: **Medium**

36. *Answer choices:*

(see index for correct answer)

- a. Calibrated probability assessment
- b. Prior probability
- c. Posterior probability
- d. Posterior predictive distribution

Guidance: level 1

:: Time series analysis ::

A _____ is a series of data points indexed in time order. Most commonly, a _____ is a sequence taken at successive equally spaced points in time. Thus it is a sequence of discrete-time data. Examples of _____ are heights of ocean tides, counts of sunspots, and the daily closing value of the Dow Jones Industrial Average.

Exam Probability: **High**

37. *Answer choices:*

(see index for correct answer)

- a. Autocorrelation technique
- b. Autoregressive conditional duration

- c. Time series
- d. Linear prediction

Guidance: level 1

:: Regression analysis ::

In statistics, _____ is "the production of an analysis that corresponds too closely or exactly to a particular set of data, and may therefore fail to fit additional data or predict future observations reliably". An overfitted model is a statistical model that contains more parameters than can be justified by the data. The essence of _____ is to have unknowingly extracted some of the residual variation as if that variation represented underlying model structure.

Exam Probability: **Medium**

38. *Answer choices:*

(see index for correct answer)

- a. Policy capturing
- b. Radial basis function network
- c. Overfitting
- d. Isotonic regression

Guidance: level 1

:: Econometrics journals ::

_____ is a peer-reviewed academic journal of economics, publishing articles in many areas of economics, especially econometrics. It is published by Wiley-Blackwell on behalf of the Econometric Society. The current editor-in-chief is Joel Sobel.

Exam Probability: **Low**

39. *Answer choices:*

(see index for correct answer)

- a. The Review of Economics and Statistics
- b. Journal of Econometrics
- c. Applied Econometrics and International Development
- d. Econometrica

Guidance: level 1

:: Hypothesis testing ::

In statistical hypothesis testing, a result has _____ when it is very unlikely to have occurred given the null hypothesis. More precisely, a study's defined significance level, denoted a, is the probability of the study rejecting the null hypothesis, given that the null hypothesis were true; and the p-value of a result, p, is the probability of obtaining a result at least as extreme, given that the null hypothesis were true. The result is statistically significant, by the standards of the study, when p < a. The significance level for a study is chosen before data collection, and typically set to 5% or much lower, depending on the field of study.

Exam Probability: **High**

40. *Answer choices:*

(see index for correct answer)

- a. Generalized p-value
- b. Uniformly most powerful test
- c. Per-comparison error rate
- d. Statistical significance

Guidance: level 1

:: Price indices ::

A _____ is a normalized average of price relatives for a given class of goods or services in a given region, during a given interval of time. It is a statistic designed to help to compare how these price relatives, taken as a whole, differ between time periods or geographical locations.

41. *Answer choices:*

(see index for correct answer)

- a. Prices received index
- b. Producer Price Index
- c. Higher Education Price Index
- d. United States Chained Consumer Price Index

Guidance: level 1

:: Data analysis ::

_____ are data formed by aggregating individual observations of a variable into groups, so that a frequency distribution of these groups serves as a convenient means of summarizing or analyzing the data.

42. *Answer choices:*

(see index for correct answer)

- a. Data thinking
- b. Ratio estimator
- c. Grouped data
- d. Text mining

:: Types of functions ::

In mathematics, a function f from a set X to a set Y is _____ , or a surjection, if for every element y in the codomain Y of f there is at least one element x in the domain X of f such that f = y. It is not required that x be unique; the function f may map one or more elements of X to the same element of Y.

Exam Probability: **High**

43. *Answer choices:*

(see index for correct answer)

- a. One-to-one correspondence
- b. Surjective
- c. Monotonic
- d. weighted

:: Sampling (statistics) ::

A _____ is the procedure of systematically acquiring and recording information about the members of a given population. The term is used mostly in connection with national population and housing _____ es; other common _____ es include agriculture, business, and traffic _____ es. The United Nations defines the essential features of population and housing _____ es as "individual enumeration, universality within a defined territory, simultaneity and defined periodicity", and recommends that population _____ es be taken at least every 10 years. United Nations recommendations also cover _____ topics to be collected, official definitions, classifications and other useful information to co-ordinate international practice.

Exam Probability: **Medium**

44. *Answer choices:*

(see index for correct answer)

- a. Census
- b. Sample
- c. Eigenpoll
- d. Sampling design

Guidance: level 1

:: Order theory ::

In mathematics, especially in order theory, an upper bound of a subset S of some partially ordered set is an element of K which is greater than or equal to every element of S. The term _____ is defined dually as an element of K which is less than or equal to every element of S. A set with an upper bound is said to be bounded from above by that bound, a set with a _____ is said to be bounded from below by that bound. The terms bounded above are also used in the mathematical literature for sets that have upper bounds.

Exam Probability: **Low**

45. *Answer choices:*

(see index for correct answer)

- a. Infimum
- b. greatest lower bound
- c. Lower bound
- d. infima

Guidance: level 1

:: Statistical data coding ::

In communications and information processing, _____ is a system of rules to convert information—such as a letter, word, sound, image, or gesture—into another form or representation, sometimes shortened or secret, for communication through a communication channel or storage in a storage medium. An early example is the invention of language, which enabled a person, through speech, to communicate what they saw, heard, felt, or thought to others. But speech limits the range of communication to the distance a voice can carry, and limits the audience to those present when the speech is uttered. The invention of writing, which converted spoken language into visual symbols, extended the range of communication across space and time.

Exam Probability: **Medium**

46. *Answer choices:*

(see index for correct answer)

- a. SIREN code
- b. Nomenclature of Territorial Units for Statistics
- c. SDMX
- d. Top-coded

Guidance: level 1

:: Statistical charts and diagrams ::

A _____ is a thematic map in which areas are shaded or patterned in proportion to the measurement of the statistical variable being displayed on the map, such as population density or per-capita income.

47. *Answer choices:*

(see index for correct answer)

- a. Control chart
- b. Control limits
- c. P-chart
- d. Violin plot

Guidance: level 1

:: Seasonality ::

In time series data, _____ is the presence of variations that occur at specific regular intervals less than a year, such as weekly, monthly, or quarterly. _____ may be caused by various factors, such as weather, vacation, and holidays and consists of periodic, repetitive, and generally regular and predictable patterns in the levels of a time series.

Exam Probability: **High**

48. *Answer choices:*

(see index for correct answer)

- a. Seasonal effects on suicide rates
- b. Seasonality

- c. Seasonal adjustment
- d. Seasonally adjusted annual rate

Guidance: level 1

:: Financial risk ::

All businesses take risks based on two factors: the probability an adverse circumstance will come about and the cost of such adverse circumstance.Risk management is the study of how to control risks and balance the possibility of gains.

Exam Probability: **Low**

49. *Answer choices:*

(see index for correct answer)

- a. Government risk
- b. Systematic risk
- c. Operational risk management
- d. Market risk

Guidance: level 1

:: Statistical tests ::

In statistics, _____ is a technique that can be used to compare means of two or more samples . This technique can be used only for numerical response data, the "Y", usually one variable, and numerical or categorical input data, the "X", always one variable, hence "one-way".

Exam Probability: **High**

50. *Answer choices:*

(see index for correct answer)

- a. Lagrange multiplier test
- b. Wald test
- c. One-way analysis of variance
- d. False positive rate

Guidance: level 1

:: Mathematical finance ::

In economics and finance, _____ , also known as present discounted value, is the value of an expected income stream determined as of the date of valuation. The _____ is always less than or equal to the future value because money has interest-earning potential, a characteristic referred to as the time value of money, except during times of negative interest rates, when the _____ will be more than the future value. Time value can be described with the simplified phrase, "A dollar today is worth more than a dollar tomorrow". Here, `worth more` means that its value is greater. A dollar today is worth more than a dollar tomorrow because the dollar can be invested and earn a day`s worth of interest, making the total accumulate to a value more than a dollar by tomorrow. Interest can be compared to rent. Just as rent is paid to a landlord by a tenant without the ownership of the asset being transferred, interest is paid to a lender by a borrower who gains access to the money for a time before paying it back. By letting the borrower have access to the money, the lender has sacrificed the exchange value of this money, and is compensated for it in the form of interest. The initial amount of the borrowed funds is less than the total amount of money paid to the lender.

Exam Probability: **Low**

51. *Answer choices:*

(see index for correct answer)

- a. No-arbitrage bounds
- b. Present value
- c. QuantLib
- d. Implied repo rate

Guidance: level 1

:: Data collection ::

_____ is information that either does not have a pre-defined data model or is not organized in a pre-defined manner. Unstructured information is typically text-heavy, but may contain data such as dates, numbers, and facts as well. This results in irregularities and ambiguities that make it difficult to understand using traditional programs as compared to data stored in fielded form in databases or annotated in documents.

Exam Probability: **Low**

52. *Answer choices:*

(see index for correct answer)

- a. Field recording
- b. Unstructured data
- c. Guardian
- d. Administrative error

Guidance: level 1

:: Mathematical and quantitative methods (economics) ::

In mathematics, a _____ is a function defined on a family of sets and taking vector values satisfying certain properties. It is a generalization of the concept of finite measure, which takes nonnegative real values only.

Exam Probability: **Medium**

53. *Answer choices:*

(see index for correct answer)

- a. Lagrange function
- b. Dual problem
- c. Lagrange multiplier
- d. Linear programming

Guidance: level 1

:: Regression analysis ::

_____ is a category of regression analysis in which the predictor does not take a predetermined form but is constructed according to information derived from the data. _____ requires larger sample sizes than regression based on parametric models because the data must supply the model structure as well as the model estimates.

Exam Probability: **Low**

54. *Answer choices:*

(see index for correct answer)

- a. Multiple correlation
- b. Growth curve
- c. Nonparametric regression
- d. Antecedent variable

:: Philosophy of science ::

An _____ definition is the articulation of _____ ization used in defining the terms of a process needed to determine the nature of an item or phenomenon and its properties such as duration, quantity, extension in space, chemical composition, etc. Since the degree of _____ ization can vary itself, it can result in a more or less _____ definition. The procedures included in definitions should be repeatable by anyone or at least by peers.

Exam Probability: **Medium**

55. *Answer choices:*

(see index for correct answer)

- a. Explanandum
- b. Organicism
- c. Operational
- d. Models of scientific inquiry

:: Loss functions ::

In mathematical optimization, statistics, econometrics, decision theory, machine learning and computational neuroscience, a loss function or cost function is a function that maps an event or values of one or more variables onto a real number intuitively representing some "cost" associated with the event. An optimization problem seeks to minimize a loss function. An _____ is either a loss function or its negative , in which case it is to be maximized.

Exam Probability: **Low**

56. *Answer choices:*

(see index for correct answer)

- a. Mean squared error
- b. Sum of absolute transformed differences
- c. Huber loss function
- d. Hinge loss

Guidance: level 1

:: Bayesian statistics ::

_____ is a theory in the field of statistics based on the Bayesian interpretation of probability where probability expresses a degree of belief in an event, which can change as new information is gathered, rather than a fixed value based upon frequency or propensity. The degree of belief may be based on prior knowledge about the event, such as the results of previous experiments, or on personal beliefs about the event. This differs from a number of other interpretations of probability, such as the frequentist interpretation that views probability as the limit of the relative frequency of an event after a large number of trials.

Exam Probability: **Medium**

57. *Answer choices:*

(see index for correct answer)

- a. Expectation propagation
- b. Bayesian statistics
- c. Marginal likelihood
- d. Bayesian approaches to brain function

Guidance: level 1

:: Non-parametric statistics ::

In statistical theory, a _____ is a class of statistics that is especially important in estimation theory; the letter "U" stands for unbiased. In elementary statistics, _____ s arise naturally in producing minimum-variance unbiased estimators.

58. *Answer choices:*

(see index for correct answer)

- a. Median test
- b. Van der Waerden test
- c. L-estimator
- d. U-statistic

Guidance: level 1

:: Consumer theory ::

In microeconomics, the _____ gives the minimum amount of money an individual needs to spend to achieve some level of utility, given a utility function and the prices of the available goods.

Exam Probability: **Low**

59. *Answer choices:*

(see index for correct answer)

- a. Expenditure function
- b. Delayed gratification
- c. Engel's law
- d. Consumer adoption of technological innovations

Guidance: level 1

Microeconomics

Microeconomics analyzes basic elements in the economy, including individual agents and markets, their interactions, and the outcomes of interactions. Individual agents may include, for example, households, firms, buyers, and sellers.

:: Asymmetric information ::

_____ is a term commonly used in economics, insurance, and risk management that describes a situation where market participation is affected by asymmetric information. When buyers and sellers have different information, it is known as a state of asymmetric information. Traders with better private information about the quality of a product will selectively participate in trades which benefit them the most, at the expense of the other trader. A textbook example is Akerlof's market for lemons.

Exam Probability: **Medium**

1. *Answer choices:*

(see index for correct answer)

- a. Adverse selection
- b. Single-crossing
- c. Credence good
- d. Principal

Guidance: level 1

:: Economics models ::

In economics, a model is a theoretical construct representing economic processes by a set of variables and a set of logical and/or quantitative relationships between them. The _____ is a simplified, often mathematical, framework designed to illustrate complex processes. Frequently, _____ s posit structural parameters. A model may have various exogenous variables, and those variables may change to create various responses by economic variables. Methodological uses of models include investigation, theorizing, and fitting theories to the world.

Exam Probability: **Medium**

2. *Answer choices:*

(see index for correct answer)

- a. Economic model
- b. Triangle model
- c. Representative agent
- d. Large-scale macroeconometric model

Guidance: level 1

:: Great Recession ::

The _____ was a period of general economic decline observed in world markets during the late 2000s and early 2010s. The scale and timing of the recession varied from country to country . The International Monetary Fund has concluded that it had the most severe economic and financial meltdown ever since the Great Depression and it is frequently seen as the second worst downturn of all time.

3. *Answer choices:*

(see index for correct answer)

- a. Great Recession
- b. AIG bonus payments controversy
- c. Thomas Herndon
- d. Reserve Primary Fund

Guidance: level 1

:: Consumer theory ::

The theory of consumer choice is the branch of microeconomics that relates preferences to consumption expenditures and to consumer demand curves. It analyzes how consumers maximize the desirability of their consumption as measured by their preferences subject to limitations on their expenditures, by maximizing utility subject to a consumer budget constraint.

Exam Probability: **Medium**

4. *Answer choices:*

(see index for correct answer)

- a. Hicksian demand
- b. Walrasian demand

- c. Quality bias
- d. Slutsky equation

Guidance: level 1

:: Tax incidence ::

A _____ is a tax in which the average tax rate increases as the taxable amount increases. The term "progressive" refers to the way the tax rate progresses from low to high, with the result that a taxpayer's average tax rate is less than the person's marginal tax rate. The term can be applied to individual taxes or to a tax system as a whole; a year, multi-year, or lifetime. _____ es are imposed in an attempt to reduce the tax incidence of people with a lower ability to pay, as such taxes shift the incidence increasingly to those with a higher ability-to-pay. The opposite of a _____ is a regressive tax, where the average tax rate or burden decreases as an individual's ability to pay increases.

Exam Probability: **Medium**

5. *Answer choices:*

(see index for correct answer)

- a. regressive tax
- b. proportional tax
- c. tax incidence
- d. Progressive tax

Guidance: level 1

:: Environmental economics ::

In economics, an _____ is the cost or benefit that affects a party who did not choose to incur that cost or benefit. Externalities often occur when a product or service's price equilibrium cannot reflect the true costs and benefits of that product or service. This causes the _____ competitive equilibrium to not be a Pareto optimality.

Exam Probability: **Low**

6. *Answer choices:*

(see index for correct answer)

- a. Externality
- b. Water scarcity
- c. Trophy property
- d. Re-Define

Guidance: level 1

:: Minimum wage law ::

_____ is the body of law which prohibits employers from hiring employees or workers for less than a given hourly, daily or monthly minimum wage. More than 90% of all countries have some kind of minimum wage legislation.

7. *Answer choices:*

(see index for correct answer)

- a. Minimum wage law
- b. Fair Minimum Wage Act of 2007
- c. Minimum Wage Fixing Convention, 1970
- d. Minimum Wage Ordinance

Guidance: level 1

:: Welfare economics ::

A deadweight loss, also known as _____ or allocative inefficiency, is a loss of economic efficiency that can occur when the free market equilibrium for a good or a service is not achieved. That can be caused by monopoly pricing in the case of artificial scarcity, an externality, a tax or subsidy, or a binding price ceiling or price floor such as a minimum wage.

Exam Probability: **Medium**

8. *Answer choices:*

(see index for correct answer)

- a. Make-work job
- b. Welfarism

- c. Excess burden
- d. Laeken indicators

Guidance: level 1

:: Production economics ::

In economics, diminishing returns is the decrease in the marginal output of a production process as the amount of a single factor of production is incrementally increased, while the amounts of all other factors of production stay constant.

Exam Probability: **Low**

9. *Answer choices:*

(see index for correct answer)

- a. Hicks-neutral technical change
- b. Synergy
- c. Diminishing marginal return
- d. Multifactor productivity

Guidance: level 1

:: Tax credits ::

In economics, a _____ is a welfare system within an income tax where people earning below a certain amount receive supplemental pay from the government instead of paying taxes to the government.

Exam Probability: **Medium**

10. *Answer choices:*

(see index for correct answer)

- a. Making Work Pay tax credit
- b. earned income
- c. Nonbusiness Energy Property Tax Credit
- d. Negative income tax

Guidance: level 1

:: Microeconomics ::

_____ are "efficiencies formed by variety, not volume". For example, a gas station that sells gasoline can sell soda, milk, baked goods, etc through their customer service representatives and thus achieve gasoline companies _____ .

Exam Probability: **High**

11. *Answer choices:*

(see index for correct answer)

- a. Bliss point
- b. Isocost
- c. Temporary equilibrium method
- d. Economies of scope

Guidance: level 1

:: Demand ::

The Kinked-Demand curve theory is an economic theory regarding oligopoly and monopolistic competition. _____ was an initial attempt to explain sticky prices.

Exam Probability: **High**

12. *Answer choices:*

(see index for correct answer)

- a. Transactions demand
- b. Kinked demand
- c. Cross-price elasticity of demand
- d. Demand-led growth

Guidance: level 1

:: Demand ::

In economics, the demand curve is the graph depicting the relationship between the price of a certain commodity and the amount of it that consumers are willing and able to purchase at any given price. It is a graphic representation of a market _____ . The demand curve for all consumers together follows from the demand curve of every individual consumer: the individual demands at each price are added together, assuming independent decision-making.

Exam Probability: **Low**

13. *Answer choices:*

(see index for correct answer)

- a. Cross-price elasticity of demand
- b. Demand-pull theory
- c. Demand schedule
- d. Demand sensing

Guidance: level 1

:: Interest ::

_____ , in finance and economics, is payment from a borrower or deposit-taking financial institution to a lender or depositor of an amount above repayment of the principal sum , at a particular rate. It is distinct from a fee which the borrower may pay the lender or some third party. It is also distinct from dividend which is paid by a company to its shareholders from its profit or reserve, but not at a particular rate decided beforehand, rather on a pro rata basis as a share in the reward gained by risk taking entrepreneurs when the revenue earned exceeds the total costs.

Exam Probability: **Medium**

14. *Answer choices:*

(see index for correct answer)

- a. Capital and Interest
- b. Penal interest
- c. Interest
- d. Fisher hypothesis

Guidance: level 1

:: Microeconomics ::

In economics, _____ and economies of scale are related but different concepts that describe what happens as the scale of production increases in the long run, when all input levels including physical capital usage are variable. The concept of _____ arises in the context of a firm's production function. It explains the behavior of the rate of increase in output relative to the associated increase in the inputs in the long run. In the long run all factors of production are variable and subject to change due to a given increase in size. While economies of scale show the effect of an increased output level on unit costs, _____ focus only on the relation between input and output quantities.

Exam Probability: **Medium**

15. *Answer choices:*

(see index for correct answer)

- a. Returns to scale
- b. Dollar voting
- c. Price signal
- d. Forced rider

Guidance: level 1

:: Production economics ::

In economics _____ is a theoretical concept where all markets are in equilibrium, and all prices and quantities have fully adjusted and are in equilibrium. The _____ contrasts with the short run where there are some constraints and markets are not fully in equilibrium.

16. *Answer choices:*

(see index for correct answer)

- a. Long run
- b. Partial productivity
- c. Multifactor productivity
- d. Constant elasticity of transformation

Guidance: level 1

:: Policy ::

A _____ is a deliberate system of principles to guide decisions and achieve rational outcomes. A _____ is a statement of intent, and is implemented as a procedure or protocol. Policies are generally adopted by a governance body within an organization. Policies can assist in both subjective and objective decision making. Policies to assist in subjective decision making usually assist senior management with decisions that must be based on the relative merits of a number of factors, and as a result are often hard to test objectively, e.g. work-life balance _____ . In contrast policies to assist in objective decision making are usually operational in nature and can be objectively tested, e.g. password _____ .

17. *Answer choices:*

(see index for correct answer)

- a. Courtesy resolution
- b. Policy
- c. Asia-Pacific Network for Global Change Research
- d. Haldane principle

Guidance: level 1

:: Price controls ::

_____ are governmental restrictions on the prices that can be charged for goods and services in a market. The intent behind implementing such controls can stem from the desire to maintain affordability of goods even during shortages, and to slow inflation, or, alternatively, to ensure a minimum income for providers of certain goods or a minimum wage. There are two primary forms of price control, a price ceiling, the maximum price that can be charged, and a price floor, the minimum price that can be charged.

Exam Probability: **Medium**

18. *Answer choices:*
(see index for correct answer)

- a. Edict on Maximum Prices
- b. Socialist accumulation
- c. Price controls
- d. Flour War

Guidance: level 1

:: Economics terminology ::

In economics, _____ or just capital is a factor of production, consisting of machinery, buildings, computers, and the like. The production function takes the general form Y=f, where Y is the amount of output produced, K is the amount of capital stock used, L is the amount of labor used, and N is the amount of natural resources used. In economic theory, _____ is one of the three primary factors of production; the others are natural resources, and laborthe stock of competences embodied in the labor force. _____ is distinct from human capital, circulating capital, and financial capital. _____ is fixed capital, which is any kind of real physical asset that is not used up in the production of a product. Usually the value of land is not included in _____ as it is not a reproducible product of human activities.

Exam Probability: **Medium**

19. *Answer choices:*

(see index for correct answer)

- a. Physical capital
- b. Headcount ratio
- c. Marginal value
- d. Confusopoly

Guidance: level 1

:: Industrial policy ::

An _____ of a country, sometimes denoted IP, sometimes industrial strategy, is its official strategic effort to encourage the development and growth of all or part of the economy, often focused on all or part of the manufacturing sector. The government takes measures "aimed at improving the competitiveness and capabilities of domestic firms and promoting structural transformation." A country's infrastructure is a major enabler of the wider economy and so often has a key role in IP.

Exam Probability: **High**

20. *Answer choices:*

(see index for correct answer)

- a. Good Design Award
- b. Industrial policy
- c. Local purchasing
- d. Managed decline

Guidance: level 1

:: Welfare reform ::

_____ s are changes in the operation of a given welfare system, with the goals of reducing the number of individuals dependent on government assistance, keeping the welfare systems affordable, and assisting recipients become self-sufficient. Classical liberals, libertarians, and conservatives generally argue that welfare and other tax-funded services reduce incentives to work, exacerbate the free-rider problem, and intensify poverty. Socialists, on the other hand, generally criticize _____ because it usually minimizes the public safety net, and strengthens the capitalist economic system. _____ is constantly debated because of the varying opinions on the government's determined balance of providing guaranteed welfare benefits, and promoting self-sufficiency.

Exam Probability: **High**

21. *Answer choices:*

(see index for correct answer)

- a. Self-Sufficiency Project
- b. Workfare

Guidance: level 1

:: Tax incidence ::

In economics, _____ or tax burden is the effect of a particular tax on the distribution of economic welfare. Economists distinguish between the entities who ultimately bear the tax burden and those on whom tax is initially imposed. The tax burden measures the true economic weight of the tax, measured by the difference between real incomes or utilities before and after imposing the tax. An individuality on whom the tax is levied does not have to bear the true size of the tax. For the example of this difference, assume a firm, that contains employer and employees. The tax imposed on the employer is divided. The concept of _____ was initially brought to economists' attention by the French Physiocrats, in particular François Quesnay, who argued that the incidence of all taxation falls ultimately on landowners and is at the expense of land rent. _____ is said to "fall" upon the group that ultimately bears the burden of, or ultimately suffers a loss from, the tax. The key concept of _____ is that the _____ or tax burden does not depend on where the revenue is collected, but on the price elasticity of demand and price elasticity of supply. As a general policy matter, the _____ should not violate the principles of a desirable tax system, especially fairness and transparency.

Exam Probability: **Medium**

22. *Answer choices:*

(see index for correct answer)

- a. Tax incidence
- b. excess burden of taxation
- c. progressive tax
- d. regressive tax

Guidance: level 1

:: Energy economics ::

_____ also draws heavily on results of energy engineering, geology, political sciences, ecology etc. Recent focus of _____ includes the following issues.

Exam Probability: **Low**

23. *Answer choices:*

- a. Petrodollar warfare
- b. Heat loss due to linear thermal bridging
- c. Fossil Fuel Beta
- d. Net energy gain

Guidance: level 1

:: Economics ::

The _____ refers to the economic agent who has the sole remaining claim on an organization's net cash flows, i.e. after the deduction of precedent agents' claims, and therefore also bears the residual risk. Residual risk is defined in this context as the risk associated with differences between the stochastic inflows of assets into the organization and precedent agents' claims on the organization's cash flows. Precedeagents' claims on an organization's cash flows can consist of e.g. employees' salaries, creditors' interest or the government's taxes.

24. *Answer choices:*

(see index for correct answer)

- a. Debt: The First 5000 Years
- b. Free contract
- c. Factor market
- d. Residual claimant

Guidance: level 1

:: Market structure and pricing ::

_____ is the percentage of a market accounted for by a specific entity. In a survey of nearly 200 senior marketing managers, 67% responded that they found the revenue- "dollar _____" metric very useful, while 61% found "unit _____" very useful.

Exam Probability: **Medium**

25. *Answer choices:*

(see index for correct answer)

- a. Market share
- b. Monopolistic competition
- c. Installed base

- d. Market share analysis

Guidance: level 1

:: Business economics ::

A _____ is an individual or institution that legally owns one or more shares of stock in a public or private corporation. _____ s may be referred to as members of a corporation. Legally, a person is not a _____ in a corporation until their name and other details are entered in the corporation's register of _____ s or members.

Exam Probability: **High**

26. *Answer choices:*
(see index for correct answer)

- a. Nonprofit studies
- b. Shareholder
- c. Cost object
- d. Service innovation

Guidance: level 1

:: Microeconomics ::

_____ is an economic concept which refers to the controlling power of consumers, over the custodians of scarce resources, in what final products should be produced. Sometimes the term _____ is also used as a hypothesis that the production of goods and services is determined by the consumers' demand.

Exam Probability: **High**

27. *Answer choices:*

(see index for correct answer)

- a. Income in kind
- b. Benefit principle
- c. Revenue Technology Services
- d. Consumption distribution

Guidance: level 1

:: United States housing bubble ::

In economics, a _____ is a business cycle contraction when there is a general decline in economic activity. Macroeconomic indicators such as GDP , investment spending, capacity utilization, household income, business profits, and inflation fall, while bankruptcies and the unemployment rate rise. In the United Kingdom, it is defined as a negative economic growth for two consecutive quarters.

Exam Probability: **Medium**

Answer choices:

(see index for correct answer)

- a. subprime loans
- b. Predatory mortgage servicing
- c. United States housing bubble
- d. Hardest Hit Fund

Guidance: level 1

:: Microeconomics ::

In economics, _____ is the comparison of two different economic outcomes, before and after a change in some underlying exogenous parameter.

Exam Probability: **High**

29. *Answer choices:*

(see index for correct answer)

- a. Isocost
- b. Comparative statics
- c. Shutdown
- d. Minimum efficient scale

Guidance: level 1

:: Economic efficiency ::

In microeconomics, _____ is, roughly speaking, a situation in which nothing can be improved without something else being hurt. Depending on the context, it is usually one of the following two related concepts.

Exam Probability: **Medium**

30. *Answer choices:*

(see index for correct answer)

- a. Memo motion
- b. Business cluster
- c. Cluster theory
- d. Economic efficiency

Guidance: level 1

:: Minimum wage ::

A _____ is the lowest remuneration that employers can legally pay their workers—the price floor below which workers may not sell their labor. Most countries had introduced _____ legislation by the end of the 20th century.

31. *Answer choices:*

(see index for correct answer)

- a. National Anti-Sweating League
- b. Anti-sweatshop
- c. Minimum wage

Guidance: level 1

:: Welfare economics ::

_____ is a branch of economics that uses microeconomic techniques to evaluate well-being at the aggregate level.

Exam Probability: **Medium**

32. *Answer choices:*

(see index for correct answer)

- a. Welfare economics
- b. Wikiprogress
- c. Unemployment insurance
- d. Local Authority Investigation Officers Group

:: Project management ::

In economics, _____ is the assignment of available resources to various uses. In the context of an entire economy, resources can be allocated by various means, such as markets or central planning.

Exam Probability: **High**

33. *Answer choices:*

(see index for correct answer)

- a. Cost-benefit
- b. Time horizon

:: Credit ::

_____ is the trust which allows one party to provide money or resources to another party wherein the second party does not reimburse the first party immediately , but promises either to repay or return those resources at a later date. In other words, _____ is a method of making reciprocity formal, legally enforceable, and extensible to a large group of unrelated people.

34. *Answer choices:*

(see index for correct answer)

- a. Paydex
- b. Home equity line of credit
- c. Actors Federal Credit Union
- d. Credit

Guidance: level 1

:: Auctioneering ::

An _____ is a process of buying and selling goods or services by offering them up for bid, taking bids, and then selling the item to the highest bidder. The open ascending price _____ is arguably the most common form of _____ in use today. Participants bid openly against one another, with each subsequent bid required to be higher than the previous bid. An _____ eer may announce prices, bidders may call out their bids themselves, or bids may be submitted electronically with the highest current bid publicly displayed. In a Dutch _____ , the _____ eer begins with a high asking price for some quantity of like items; the price is lowered until a participant is willing to accept the _____ eer's price for some quantity of the goods in the lot or until the seller's reserve price is met. While _____ s are most associated in the public imagination with the sale of antiques, paintings, rare collectibles and expensive wines, _____ s are also used for commodities, livestock, radio spectrum and used cars. In economic theory, an _____ may refer to any mechanism or set of trading rules for exchange.

35. *Answer choices:*

(see index for correct answer)

- a. Dutch auction
- b. Chinese auction
- c. Walton School of Auctioneering
- d. Vehicle impoundment

Guidance: level 1

:: Socioeconomics ::

Economic interventionism is an economic policy perspective favoring
_____ in the market process to correct the market failures and promote the
general welfare of the people. An economic intervention is an action taken by a
government or international institution in a market economy in an effort to
impact the economy beyond the basic regulation of fraud and enforcement of
contracts and provision of public goods. Economic intervention can be aimed at
a variety of political or economic objectives, such as promoting economic
growth, increasing employment, raising wages, raising or reducing prices,
promoting income equality, managing the money supply and interest rates,
increasing profits, or addressing market failures.

Exam Probability: **High**

36. *Answer choices:*

(see index for correct answer)

- a. Government intervention
- b. purchasing power
- c. International Day for the Eradication of Poverty
- d. Horatio Alger myth

Guidance: level 1

:: Inflation ::

_____ is a sustained increase in the general price level of goods and services in an economy over a period of time. When the general price level rises, each unit of currency buys fewer goods and services; consequently, _____ reflects a reduction in the purchasing power per unit of money a loss of real value in the medium of exchange and unit of account within the economy. The measure of _____ is the _____ rate, the annualized percentage change in a general price index, usually the consumer price index, over time. The opposite of _____ is deflation.

Exam Probability: **High**

37. *Answer choices:*

(see index for correct answer)

- a. Inflation
- b. Inflation hedge
- c. Inflationary gap
- d. Base effect

:: Costs ::

_____ s are costs that change as the quantity of the good or service that a business produces changes. _____ s are the sum of marginal costs over all units produced. They can also be considered normal costs. Fixed costs and _____ s make up the two components of total cost. Direct costs are costs that can easily be associated with a particular cost object. However, not all _____ s are direct costs. For example, variable manufacturing overhead costs are _____ s that are indirect costs, not direct costs. _____ s are sometimes called unit-level costs as they vary with the number of units produced.

Exam Probability: **High**

38. *Answer choices:*

(see index for correct answer)

- a. Semi-variable cost
- b. Manufacturing cost
- c. Average variable cost
- d. Spare part

:: Renewable resources ::

A _____ is a natural resource which will replenish to replace the portion depleted by usage and consumption, either through natural reproduction or other recurring processes in a finite amount of time in a human time scale. _____ s are a part of Earth's natural environment and the largest components of its ecosphere. A positive life cycle assessment is a key indicator of a resource's sustainability.

Exam Probability: **Medium**

39. *Answer choices:*

(see index for correct answer)

- a. renewable
- b. Proteak
- c. Cardboard bicycle
- d. Renewable resource

Guidance: level 1

:: Intertemporal economics ::

_____ is income not spent, or deferred consumption. Methods of _____ include putting money aside in, for example, a deposit account, a pension account, an investment fund, or as cash. _____ also involves reducing expenditures, such as recurring costs. In terms of personal finance, _____ generally specifies low-risk preservation of money, as in a deposit account, versus investment, wherein risk is a lot higher; in economics more broadly, it refers to any income not used for immediate consumption.

40. *Answer choices:*

(see index for correct answer)

- a. Intertemporal consumption
- b. Liquidity constraint
- c. Intertemporal equilibrium
- d. Saving

Guidance: level 1

:: Corporate finance ::

The _____ of a corporation is all of the shares into which ownership of the corporation is divided. In American English, the shares are commonly known as "_____ s". A single share of the _____ represents fractional ownership of the corporation in proportion to the total number of shares. This typically entitles the _____ holder to that fraction of the company's earnings, proceeds from liquidation of assets , or voting power, often dividing these up in proportion to the amount of money each _____ holder has invested. Not all _____ is necessarily equal, as certain classes of _____ may be issued for example without voting rights, with enhanced voting rights, or with a certain priority to receive profits or liquidation proceeds before or after other classes of shareholders.

Exam Probability: **Medium**

41. *Answer choices:*

(see index for correct answer)

- a. Capital structure
- b. Stock
- c. Thin capitalisation rules
- d. Common stock

Guidance: level 1

:: Income ::

_____ is the consumption and saving opportunity gained by an entity within a specified timeframe, which is generally expressed in monetary terms. For households and individuals, " _____ is the sum of all the wages, salaries, profits, interest payments, rents, and other forms of earnings received in a given period of time."

Exam Probability: **Medium**

42. *Answer choices:*

(see index for correct answer)

- a. Giganomics
- b. Income
- c. Salary inversion
- d. average income

:: Markets (customer bases) ::

_____ is the traditional concept of economic equilibrium, appropriate for the analysis of commodity markets with flexible prices and many traders, and serving as the benchmark of efficiency in economic analysis. It relies crucially on the assumption of a competitive environment where each trader decides upon a quantity that is so small compared to the total quantity traded in the market that their individual transactions have no influence on the prices. Competitive markets are an ideal standard by which other market structures are evaluated.

Exam Probability: **Low**

43. *Answer choices:*

(see index for correct answer)

- a. Competitive equilibrium
- b. Captive market
- c. Walrasian equilibrium
- d. Economic equilibrium

:: Goods ::

In economics, an _____ is a good whose demand decreases when consumer income rises , unlike normal goods, for which the opposite is observed. Normal goods are those goods for which the demand rises as consumer income rises. This would be the opposite of a superior good, one that is often associated with wealth and the wealthy, whereas an _____ is associated with lower socio-economic groups.

Exam Probability: **High**

44. *Answer choices:*

(see index for correct answer)

- a. Fast-moving consumer goods
- b. Experience good
- c. Inferior good
- d. Case

Guidance: level 1

:: Production economics ::

In economics and in particular neoclassical economics, the _____ or marginal physical productivity of an input is the change in output resulting from employing one more unit of a particular input , assuming that the quantities of other inputs are kept constant.

Exam Probability: **Medium**

45. *Answer choices:*

- a. Marginal product of labor
- b. Constant elasticity of transformation
- c. Marginal product
- d. Division of work

Guidance: level 1

:: Economic growth ::

_____ describes various measures of the efficiency of production. Often , a _____ measure is expressed as the ratio of an aggregate output to a single input or an aggregate input used in a production process, i.e. output per unit of input. Most common example is the labour _____ measure, e.g., such as GDP per worker. There are many different definitions of _____ and the choice among them depends on the purpose of the _____ measurement and/or data availability. The key source of difference between various _____ measures is also usually related to how the outputs and the inputs are aggregated into scalars to obtain such a ratio-type measure of _____ .

Exam Probability: **Low**

46. *Answer choices:*

- a. Inada conditions

- b. Zero growth
- c. Productivity
- d. Economic growth

Guidance: level 1

:: Bankruptcy ::

_____ is a legal process through which people or other entities who cannot repay debts to creditors may seek relief from some or all of their debts. In most jurisdictions, _____ is imposed by a court order, often initiated by the debtor.

Exam Probability: **Low**

47. *Answer choices:*

(see index for correct answer)

- a. Bankruptcy
- b. Unsecured creditor
- c. Enterprise Turnaround Initiative Corporation of Japan
- d. Petition mill

Guidance: level 1

:: Economics terminology ::

In economics, an externality is the cost or benefit that affects a party who did not choose to incur that cost or benefit. Externalities often occur when a product or service's price equilibrium cannot reflect the true costs and benefits of that product or service. This causes the externality competitive equilibrium to not be a Pareto optimality.

Exam Probability: **High**

48. *Answer choices:*

(see index for correct answer)

- a. Overnight trade
- b. External cost
- c. Marginal value
- d. Economic catalyst

Guidance: level 1

:: Production economics ::

In economic theory, a _____ is the unit cost of using a factor of production, such as labor or physical capital.

Exam Probability: **Low**

49. *Answer choices:*

(see index for correct answer)

- a. Indirect cost
- b. Theory of non-constraint
- c. Fragmentation
- d. Factor price

Guidance: level 1

:: Health economics ::

In an insurance policy, the _____ is the amount paidout of pocket by the policy holder before an insurance provider will pay any expenses. In general usage, the term _____ may be used to describe one of several types of clauses that are used by insurance companies as a threshold for policy payments.

Exam Probability: **Medium**

50. *Answer choices:*

(see index for correct answer)

- a. Social determinants of health in poverty
- b. Cost-effectiveness analysis
- c. Lives at Risk
- d. Centre for Reviews and Dissemination

Guidance: level 1

:: Termination of employment ::

_____ is the withdrawal from one's position or occupation or from one's active working life. A person may also semi-retire by reducing work hours.

51. *Answer choices:*
(see index for correct answer)

- a. Resignation
- b. Dismissal
- c. Retirement
- d. Luis Gabriel Aguilera

Guidance: level 1

:: Production economics ::

In economics long run is a theoretical concept where all markets are in equilibrium, and all prices and quantities have fully adjusted and are in equilibrium. The long run contrasts with the _____ where there are some constraints and markets are not fully in equilibrium.

52. *Answer choices:*

(see index for correct answer)

- a. Hicks-neutral technical change
- b. HMI quality
- c. Total factor productivity
- d. Short run

Guidance: level 1

:: Microeconomics ::

In economics and business decision-making, a sunk cost is a cost that has already been incurred and cannot be recovered.

Exam Probability: **High**

53. *Answer choices:*

(see index for correct answer)

- a. Marginal factor cost
- b. Price signal
- c. Repugnancy costs
- d. Yield management

Guidance: level 1

:: Anti-globalization ::

A _____ , underground economy, or shadow economy is a clandestine market or series of transactions that has some aspect of illegality or is characterized by some form of noncompliant behavior with an institutional set of rules. If the rule defines the set of goods and services whose production and distribution is prohibited by law, non-compliance with the rule constitutes a _____ trade since the transaction itself is illegal. Parties engaging in the production or distribution of prohibited goods and services are members of the illegal economy. Examples include the drug trade, prostitution , illegal currency transactions and human trafficking. Violations of the tax code involving income tax evasion constitute membership in the unreported economy.

Exam Probability: **Medium**

54. *Answer choices:*

(see index for correct answer)

- a. China Compulsory Certificate
- b. Food sovereignty
- c. Global citizens movement
- d. World Social Forum

Guidance: level 1

:: Scarcity ::

A _____ , also known as excess burden or allocative inefficiency, is a loss of economic efficiency that can occur when the free market equilibrium for a good or a service is not achieved. That can be caused by monopoly pricing in the case of artificial scarcity, an externality, a tax or subsidy, or a binding price ceiling or price floor such as a minimum wage.

Exam Probability: **High**

55. *Answer choices:*

(see index for correct answer)

- a. Scarcity value
- b. Deadweight loss
- c. Economic rent
- d. Thoughts and Details on Scarcity

Guidance: level 1

:: Monopoly (economics) ::

A _____ exists when a specific person or enterprise is the only supplier of a particular commodity. This contrasts with a monopsony which relates to a single entity's control of a market to purchase a good or service, and with oligopoly which consists of a few sellers dominating a market. Monopolies are thus characterized by a lack of economic competition to produce the good or service, a lack of viable substitute goods, and the possibility of a high _____ price well above the seller's marginal cost that leads to a high _____ profit. The verb monopolise or monopolize refers to the process by which a company gains the ability to raise prices or exclude competitors. In economics, a _____ is a single seller. In law, a _____ is a business entity that has significant market power, that is, the power to charge overly high prices. Although monopolies may be big businesses, size is not a characteristic of a _____ . A small business may still have the power to raise prices in a small industry .

Exam Probability: **Medium**

56. *Answer choices:*

(see index for correct answer)

- a. History of monopoly
- b. Bilateral monopoly
- c. Monopoly
- d. Complementary monopoly

Guidance: level 1

:: Demand ::

Price _____ is a measure used in economics to show the responsiveness, or elasticity, of the quantity demanded of a good or service to a change in its price when nothing but the price changes. More precisely, it gives the percentage change in quantity demanded in response to a one percent change in price.

Exam Probability: **Low**

57. *Answer choices:*

(see index for correct answer)

- a. Wealth elasticity of demand
- b. Supply creates its own demand
- c. Elasticity of demand
- d. price elasticity

Guidance: level 1

:: Economics terminology ::

_____ is the total receipts a seller can obtain from selling goods or services to buyers. It can be written as P × Q, which is the price of the goods multiplied by the quantity of the sold goods.

Exam Probability: **Medium**

58. *Answer choices:*

(see index for correct answer)

- a. Price variance
- b. federal funds
- c. Total revenue
- d. Order condition

Guidance: level 1

:: National accounts ::

A _____ is monetary compensation paid by an employer to an employee in exchange for work done. Payment may be calculated as a fixed amount for each task completed , or at an hourly or daily rate , or based on an easily measured quantity of work done.

Exam Probability: **High**

59. *Answer choices:*

(see index for correct answer)

- a. Wage
- b. Fixed capital
- c. Savings identity
- d. Net output

Guidance: level 1

Macroeconomics and monetary economics

Macroeconomics analyzes the entire economy (meaning aggregated production, consumption, savings, and investment) and issues affecting it, including unemployment of resources (labour, capital, and land), inflation, economic growth, and the public policies that address these issues (monetary, fiscal, and other policies).

:: Operations research ::

_____ or stock is the goods and materials that a business holds for the ultimate goal of resale .

Exam Probability: **Low**

1. *Answer choices:*

- a. Dynamic simulation
- b. Algorithm design
- c. Inventory
- d. Nuffield Tools and Gauges

Guidance: level 1

:: Inflation ::

The _____ is the rate of interest an investor, saver or lender receives after allowing for inflation. It can be described more formally by the Fisher equation, which states that the _____ is approximately the nominal interest rate minus the inflation rate.

Exam Probability: **Low**

2. *Answer choices:*

- a. Real interest rate
- b. Zero stroke
- c. Whip inflation now
- d. Stealth inflation

Guidance: level 1

:: Unemployment ::

_____ is a form of involuntary unemployment caused by a mismatch between the skills that workers in the economy can offer, and the skills demanded of workers by employers . _____ is often brought about by technological changes that make the job skills of many workers obsolete.

Exam Probability: **Low**

3. *Answer choices:*

(see index for correct answer)

- a. Mount Street Club
- b. natural rate of unemployment
- c. Structural unemployment
- d. Short time

Guidance: level 1

:: Collective investment schemes ::

A _____ is a professionally managed investment fund that pools money from many investors to purchase securities. These investors may be retail or institutional in nature.

4. *Answer choices:*

(see index for correct answer)

- a. Mutual fund
- b. Unitised insurance fund
- c. Common fund
- d. collective Investment

Guidance: level 1

:: Economics laws ::

The _____ is a fundamental principle of economic theory which states that, keeping other factors constant, an increase in price results in an increase in quantity supplied. In other words, there is a direct relationship between price and quantity: quantities respond in the same direction as price changes. This means that producers are willing to offer more of a product for sale on the market at higher prices by increasing production as a way of increasing profits.

Exam Probability: **Medium**

5. *Answer choices:*

(see index for correct answer)

- a. Gibrat's law

- b. Law of reflux
- c. Law of supply
- d. Iron law of prohibition

Guidance: level 1

:: Financial markets ::

A _____ is a market in which people trade financial securities and derivatives such as futures and options at low transaction costs. Securities include stocks and bonds, and precious metals.

Exam Probability: **Low**

6. *Answer choices:*

(see index for correct answer)

- a. Financial market
- b. Virtual bidding
- c. Bond fund
- d. Over-the-counter

Guidance: level 1

:: Central banks ::

A _____ , reserve bank, or monetary authority is the institution that manages the currency, money supply, and interest rates of a state or formal monetary union,and oversees their commercial banking system. In contrast to a commercial bank, a _____ possesses a monopoly on increasing the monetary base in the state, and also generally controls the printing/coining of the national currency, which serves as the state's legal tender. A _____ also acts as a lender of last resort to the banking sector during times of financial crisis. Most _____ s also have supervisory and regulatory powers to ensure the solvency of member institutions, to prevent bank runs, and to discourage reckless or fraudulent behavior by member banks.

Exam Probability: **Medium**

7. *Answer choices:*

(see index for correct answer)

- a. Central Bank of Nicaragua
- b. Central bank
- c. Central Bank of Brazil
- d. Bank of Albania

Guidance: level 1

:: Investment ::

_____ is a component of gross domestic product . What is produced in a certain country is naturally also sold eventually, but some of the goods produced in a given year may be sold in a later year rather than in the year they were produced. Conversely, some of the goods sold in a given year might have been produced in an earlier year. The difference between goods produced and goods sold in a given year is called _____ . The concept can be applied to the economy as a whole or to an individual firm.

Exam Probability: **High**

8. *Answer choices:*

(see index for correct answer)

- a. Investment theory
- b. China International Fair for Investment and Trade
- c. Inventory investment
- d. Disinvestment

Guidance: level 1

:: Monetary economics ::

_____ is any item or verifiable record that is generally accepted as payment for goods and services and repayment of debts, such as taxes, in a particular country or socio-economic context. The main functions of _____ are distinguished as: a medium of exchange, a unit of account, a store of value and sometimes, a standard of deferred payment. Any item or verifiable record that fulfils these functions can be considered as _____ .

9. *Answer choices:*

(see index for correct answer)

- a. Money
- b. vault Cash
- c. Quantum economics
- d. Asset price channel

Guidance: level 1

:: Capitalism ::

A _____ , equity market or share market is the aggregation of buyers and sellers of stocks , which represent ownership claims on businesses; these may include securities listed on a public stock exchange, as well as stock that is only traded privately. Examples of the latter include shares of private companies which are sold to investors through equity crowdfunding platforms. Stock exchanges list shares of common equity as well as other security types, e.g. corporate bonds and convertible bonds.

Exam Probability: **Medium**

10. *Answer choices:*

(see index for correct answer)

- a. Stock market

- b. State monopoly capitalism
- c. Welfare capitalism
- d. Social market economy

Guidance: level 1

:: Unemployment ::

The _____ is the name that was given to a key concept in the study of economic activity. Milton Friedman and Edmund Phelps, tackling this `human` problem in the 1960s, both received the Nobel Prize in economics for their work, and the development of the concept is cited as a main motivation behind the prize. A simplistic summary of the concept is: `The _____ , when an economy is in a steady state of "full employment", is the proportion of the workforce who are unemployed`. Put another way, this concept clarifies that the economic term "full employment" does not mean "zero unemployment". It represents the hypothetical unemployment rate consistent with aggregate production being at the "long-run" level. This level is consistent with aggregate production in the absence of various temporary frictions such as incomplete price adjustment in labor and goods markets. The _____ therefore corresponds to the unemployment rate prevailing under a classical view of determination of activity.

Exam Probability: **Low**

11. *Answer choices:*

(see index for correct answer)

- a. Natural rate of unemployment
- b. Outplacement

- c. Short time
- d. Overqualification

Guidance: level 1

:: Export ::

An _____ in international trade is a good or service produced in one country that is bought by someone in another country. The seller of such goods and services is an _____ er; the foreign buyer is an importer.

Exam Probability: **Medium**

12. *Answer choices:*

(see index for correct answer)

- a. Live export
- b. Export variants of Soviet military equipment
- c. Export hay

Guidance: level 1

:: Economics ::

_____ is the process in which a nation is being improved in the sector of the economic, political, and social well-being of its people. The term has been used frequently by economists, politicians, and others in the 20th and 21st centuries. The concept, however, has been in existence in the West for centuries. "Modernization, "westernization", and especially "industrialization" are other terms often used while discussing _____ . _____ has a direct relationship with the environment and environmental issues. _____ is very often confused with industrial development, even in some academic sources.

Exam Probability: **Low**

13. *Answer choices:*

(see index for correct answer)

- a. Productive efficiency
- b. Economic development
- c. Economics of science
- d. Labor demand

Guidance: level 1

:: Socioeconomics ::

_____ is the amount of goods and services that can be purchased with a unit of currency. For example, if one had taken one unit of currency to a store in the 1950s, it would have been possible to buy a greater number of items than would be the case today, indicating that the currency had a greater _____ in the 1950s. Currency can be either a commodity money, like gold or silver, or fiat money emitted by government sanctioned agencies.

Exam Probability: **High**

14. *Answer choices:*

(see index for correct answer)

- a. Gratuity
- b. Literacy
- c. Analytical Center for the Government of the Russian Federation
- d. Class analysis

Guidance: level 1

:: Economics curves ::

In microeconomics, _____ is an economic model of price determination in a market. It postulates that, holding all else equal, in a competitive market, the unit price for a particular good, or other traded item such as labor or liquid financial assets, will vary until it settles at a point where the quantity demanded will equal the quantity supplied , resulting in an economic equilibrium for price and quantity transacted.

15. *Answer choices:*

(see index for correct answer)

- a. Hubbert curve
- b. Expectation hypothesis
- c. Great Gatsby curve
- d. Wage curve

Guidance: level 1

:: Credit ::

_____ is the trust which allows one party to provide money or resources to another party wherein the second party does not reimburse the first party immediately , but promises either to repay or return those resources at a later date. In other words, _____ is a method of making reciprocity formal, legally enforceable, and extensible to a large group of unrelated people.

16. *Answer choices:*

(see index for correct answer)

- a. Credit
- b. Package loan

- c. Debt validation
- d. Credit history

Guidance: level 1

:: Goods ::

In most contexts, the concept of _____ denotes the conduct that should be preferred when posed with a choice between possible actions. _____ is generally considered to be the opposite of evil, and is of interest in the study of morality, ethics, religion and philosophy. The specific meaning and etymology of the term and its associated translations among ancient and contemporary languages show substantial variation in its inflection and meaning depending on circumstances of place, history, religious, or philosophical context.

Exam Probability: **Low**

17. *Answer choices:*
(see index for correct answer)

- a. Superior good
- b. Good
- c. Cargo
- d. Free good

Guidance: level 1

:: Microeconomics ::

In economics and related disciplines, a _____ is a cost in making any economic trade when participating in a market.

Exam Probability: **Medium**

18. *Answer choices:*

(see index for correct answer)

- a. Marginal cost
- b. Necessity good
- c. Excess supply
- d. National Competition Policy

Guidance: level 1

:: Economic problems ::

The causes of _____ are heavily debated. Classical economics, new classical economics, and the Austrian School of economics argued that market mechanisms are reliable means of resolving _____ . These theories argue against interventions imposed on the labor market from the outside, such as unionization, bureaucratic work rules, minimum wage laws, taxes, and other regulations that they claim discourage the hiring of workers. Keynesian economics emphasizes the cyclical nature of _____ and recommends government interventions in the economy that it claims will reduce _____ during recessions. This theory focuses on recurrent shocks that suddenly reduce aggregate demand for goods and services and thus reduce demand for workers. Keynesian models recommend government interventions designed to increase demand for workers; these can include financial stimuli, publicly funded job creation, and expansionist monetary policies. Its namesake economist, John Maynard Keynes, believed that the root cause of _____ is the desire of investors to receive more money rather than produce more products, which is not possible without public bodies producing new money. A third group of theories emphasize the need for a stable supply of capital and investment to maintain full employment. On this view, government should guarantee full employment through fiscal policy, monetary policy and trade policy as stated, for example, in the US Employment Act of 1946, by counteracting private sector or trade investment volatility, and reducing inequality.

Exam Probability: **Medium**

19. *Answer choices:*

(see index for correct answer)

- a. Unemployment
- b. Escape from Affluenza
- c. Turnaround management
- d. The Nature of Mass Poverty

Guidance: level 1

:: Economics laws ::

The _____ states that in the absence of trade frictions, and under conditions of free competition and price flexibility, identical goods sold in different locations must sell for the same price when prices are expressed in a common currency. This law is derived from the assumption of the inevitable elimination of all arbitrage.

Exam Probability: **Medium**

20. *Answer choices:*

(see index for correct answer)

- a. Walras' law
- b. The New York Pizza Connection
- c. Law of one price
- d. Gibrat's law

Guidance: level 1

:: Business cycle ::

The _____ , also known as the economic cycle or trade cycle, is the downward and upward movement of gross domestic product around its long-term growth trend. The length of a _____ is the period of time containing a single boom and contraction in sequence. These fluctuations typically involve shifts over time between periods of relatively rapid economic growth and periods of relative stagnation or decline .

Exam Probability: **Low**

21. *Answer choices:*

(see index for correct answer)

- a. Centre for International Research on Economic Tendency Surveys
- b. Economic Confidence Model
- c. Reference date
- d. Trough

Guidance: level 1

:: Money ::

_____ is money whose value comes from a commodity of which it is made. _____ consists of objects that have value in themselves as well as value in their use as money.

Exam Probability: **High**

22. *Answer choices:*

(see index for correct answer)

- a. Lump sum
- b. Money burning
- c. Nominal money
- d. Key money

Guidance: level 1

:: Gross domestic product ::

The GDP gap or the output gap is the difference between actual GDP or actual output and potential GDP. The calculation for the output gap is Y−Y* where Y is actual output and Y* is potential output. If this calculation yields a positive number it is called an inflationary gap and indicates the growth of aggregate demand is outpacing the growth of aggregate supply—possibly creating inflation; if the calculation yields a negative number it is called a _____ —possibly signifying deflation.

Exam Probability: **High**

23. *Answer choices:*

(see index for correct answer)

- a. Output gap
- b. GDP density
- c. Recessionary gap

- d. openness index

Guidance: level 1

:: Macroeconomics ::

In economics, the _____ is a metric that quantifies induced consumption, the concept that the increase in personal consumer spending occurs with an increase in disposable income . The proportion of disposable income which individuals spend on consumption is known as propensity to consume. MPC is the proportion of additional income that an individual consumes. For example, if a household earns one extra dollar of disposable income, and the _____ is 0.65, then of that dollar, the household will spend 65 cents and save 35 cents. Obviously, the household cannot spend more than the extra dollar .

Exam Probability: **Medium**

24. *Answer choices:*

(see index for correct answer)

- a. Macroeconomic policy instruments
- b. Marginal propensity to consume
- c. loanable funds market
- d. Absolute income hypothesis

Guidance: level 1

:: National accounts ::

Gross domestic product is a monetary measure of the market value of all the final goods and services produced in a period of time, often annually. GDP per capita does not, however, reflect differences in the cost of living and the inflation rates of the countries; therefore using a basis of GDP per capita at purchasing power parity is arguably more useful when comparing differences in living standards between nations.

Exam Probability: **Low**

25. *Answer choices:*

(see index for correct answer)

- a. Nominal GDP
- b. Consumption of fixed capital
- c. Personal income
- d. Export performance

Guidance: level 1

:: Production economics ::

In economics long run is a theoretical concept where all markets are in equilibrium, and all prices and quantities have fully adjusted and are in equilibrium. The long run contrasts with the _____ where there are some constraints and markets are not fully in equilibrium.

26. *Answer choices:*

(see index for correct answer)

- a. Economies of scale
- b. Productivity world
- c. Short run
- d. Theory of non-constraint

Guidance: level 1

:: Capitalist systems ::

_____ is an economic system based on the private ownership of the means of production and their operation for profit. Characteristics central to _____ include private property, capital accumulation, wage labor, voluntary exchange, a price system, and competitive markets. In a capitalist market economy, decision-making and investment are determined by every owner of wealth, property or production ability in financial and capital markets, whereas prices and the distribution of goods and services are mainly determined by competition in goods and services markets.

Exam Probability: **High**

27. *Answer choices:*

(see index for correct answer)

- a. Advanced capitalism
- b. Coordinated market economy
- c. Capitalism
- d. New economy

Guidance: level 1

:: National accounts ::

A _____ is monetary compensation paid by an employer to an employee in exchange for work done. Payment may be calculated as a fixed amount for each task completed , or at an hourly or daily rate , or based on an easily measured quantity of work done.

Exam Probability: **Medium**

28. *Answer choices:*

(see index for correct answer)

- a. Export performance
- b. Compensation of employees
- c. nominal GDP
- d. Gross national income

Guidance: level 1

:: International economics ::

In economics, a country's _____ is one of the two components of its balance of payments, the other being the capital account . The _____ consists of the balance of trade, net primary income or factor income and net cash transfers, that have taken place over a given period of time. The _____ balance is one of two major measures of a country's foreign trade . A _____ surplus indicates that the value of a country's net foreign assets grew over the period in question, and a _____ deficit indicates that it shrank. Both government and private payments are included in the calculation. It is called the _____ because goods and services are generally consumed in the current period.

Exam Probability: **Medium**

29. *Answer choices:*

(see index for correct answer)

- a. Job migration
- b. Multinational corporation
- c. Jurisdictional arbitrage
- d. Current account

Guidance: level 1

:: Underground culture ::

A black market, _____ , or shadow economy is a clandestine market or series of transactions that has some aspect of illegality or is characterized by some form of noncompliant behavior with an institutional set of rules. If the rule defines the set of goods and services whose production and distribution is prohibited by law, non-compliance with the rule constitutes a black market trade since the transaction itself is illegal. Parties engaging in the production or distribution of prohibited goods and services are members of the illegal economy. Examples include the drug trade, prostitution , illegal currency transactions and human trafficking. Violations of the tax code involving income tax evasion constitute membership in the unreported economy.

Exam Probability: **Medium**

30. *Answer choices:*

(see index for correct answer)

- a. Cabaret Voltaire
- b. Underground economy
- c. Afro-punk
- d. The Hidden Wiki

Guidance: level 1

:: International economics ::

_____ is an agreement in which one company hires another company to be responsible for a planned or existing activity that is or could be done internally,and sometimes involves transferring employees and assets from one firm to another.

31. *Answer choices:*

(see index for correct answer)

- a. Diamond model
- b. Re-exportation
- c. Remittance
- d. Financial export

Guidance: level 1

:: National accounts ::

A _____ consists of one people who live in the same dwelling and share meals. It may also consist of a single family or another group of people. A dwelling is considered to contain multiple _____ s if meals or living spaces are not shared. The _____ is the basic unit of analysis in many social, microeconomic and government models, and is important to economics and inheritance.

Exam Probability: **High**

32. *Answer choices:*

(see index for correct answer)

- a. Compensation of employees
- b. Household

- c. Gross domestic product
- d. Gross domestic income

Guidance: level 1

:: Public finance ::

_____ or expenditure includes all government consumption, investment, and transfer payments. In national income accounting the acquisition by governments of goods and services for current use, to directly satisfy the individual or collective needs of the community, is classed as government final consumption expenditure. Government acquisition of goods and services intended to create future benefits, such as infrastructure investment or research spending, is classed as government investment . These two types of _____ , on final consumption and on gross capital formation, together constitute one of the major components of gross domestic product.

Exam Probability: **High**

33. *Answer choices:*
(see index for correct answer)

- a. Certified California Municipal Treasurer
- b. Public bank
- c. Budget Day
- d. Great Lakes Higher Education Corporation

Guidance: level 1

:: Finance ::

_____ is a field that is concerned with the allocation of assets and liabilities over space and time, often under conditions of risk or uncertainty. _____ can also be defined as the art of money management. Participants in the market aim to price assets based on their risk level, fundamental value, and their expected rate of return. _____ can be split into three sub-categories: public _____ , corporate _____ and personal _____ .

Exam Probability: **High**

34. *Answer choices:*

(see index for correct answer)

- a. Test and learn
- b. Finance
- c. Orphan structure
- d. Tangible common equity

Guidance: level 1

:: Inflation ::

An _____ , in economics, is the amount by which the actual gross domestic product exceeds potential full-employment GDP. It is one type of output gap, the other being a recessionary gap.

Exam Probability: **Medium**

35. *Answer choices:*

(see index for correct answer)

- a. Inflationary spike
- b. Disinflation
- c. Inflationary gap
- d. demand-pull inflation

Guidance: level 1

:: Trade policy ::

_____ is a trade policy that does not restrict imports or exports; it can also be understood as the free market idea applied to international trade. In government, _____ is predominantly advocated by political parties that hold liberal economic positions while economically left-wing and nationalist political parties generally support protectionism, the opposite of _____ .

Exam Probability: **Low**

36. *Answer choices:*

(see index for correct answer)

- a. Free trade
- b. Free trade zone
- c. Green box policies
- d. protectionist

Guidance: level 1

:: Currency ::

In economics, _____ is one of the functions of money. The value of something is measured in a specific currency. This allows different things to compared against each other; for example, goods, services, assets, liabilities, labor, income, expenses. It lends meaning to profits, losses, liability, or assets.

Exam Probability: **High**

37. *Answer choices:*

(see index for correct answer)

- a. Currency intervention
- b. Debasement
- c. Non-decimal currency
- d. Unit of account

:: Demand ::

In economics, the demand curve is the graph depicting the relationship between the price of a certain commodity and the amount of it that consumers are willing and able to purchase at any given price. It is a graphic representation of a market _____ . The demand curve for all consumers together follows from the demand curve of every individual consumer: the individual demands at each price are added together, assuming independent decision-making.

Exam Probability: **Medium**

38. *Answer choices:*

(see index for correct answer)

- a. Effective demand
- b. Demand schedule
- c. Cross-price elasticity of demand
- d. Elasticity of demand

:: Economics ::

In economics, the _____ is the marketplace in which final goods or services are offered for purchase by businesses and the public sector. Focusing on the sale of finished goods, it does not include trading in raw or other intermediate materials.

Exam Probability: **Medium**

39. *Answer choices:*

(see index for correct answer)

- a. Product market
- b. Economics of science
- c. Profit efficiency
- d. Cash collection

Guidance: level 1

:: Economics terminology ::

In economics, _____ or just capital is a factor of production , consisting of machinery, buildings, computers, and the like. The production function takes the general form Y=f, where Y is the amount of output produced, K is the amount of capital stock used, L is the amount of labor used, and N is the amount of natural resources used. In economic theory, _____ is one of the three primary factors of production; the others are natural resources , and laborthe stock of competences embodied in the labor force. _____ is distinct from human capital , circulating capital, and financial capital. _____ is fixed capital, which is any kind of real physical asset that is not used up in the production of a product. Usually the value of land is not included in _____ as it is not a reproducible product of human activities.

Exam Probability: **Low**

40. *Answer choices:*

(see index for correct answer)

- a. Normative statement
- b. Physical capital
- c. Fungibility
- d. Electronic payment advice

Guidance: level 1

:: Marketing ::

A _____ is the quantity of payment or compensation given by one party to another in return for one unit of goods or services.. A _____ is influenced by both production costs and demand for the product. A _____ may be determined by a monopolist or may be imposed on the firm by market conditions.

Exam Probability: **High**

41. *Answer choices:*

(see index for correct answer)

- a. Fifth screen
- b. Price
- c. Buy one, get one free
- d. Marketing spending

Guidance: level 1

:: Financial crises ::

In economics, _____ is very high and typically accelerating inflation. It quickly erodes the real value of the local currency, as the prices of all goods increase. This causes people to minimize their holdings in that currency as they usually switch to more stable foreign currencies, often the US Dollar. Prices typically remain stable in terms of other relatively stable currencies.

Exam Probability: **Medium**

42. *Answer choices:*

(see index for correct answer)

- a. SsangYong Group
- b. Sovereign default
- c. Hyperinflation
- d. Crisis of 1982

Guidance: level 1

:: Official statistics ::

_____ is the exchange of capital, goods, and services across international borders or territories.

Exam Probability: **Medium**

43. *Answer choices:*

(see index for correct answer)

- a. Market production
- b. FISIM
- c. International trade
- d. DataViva

Guidance: level 1

:: Welfare state ::

Unlike the exchange transaction which mutually benefits all the parties involved in it, the _____ consists of a donor and a recipient, with the donor giving up something of value without receiving anything in return. Transfers can be made both between individuals and entities, such as a private companies or a governmental bodies. These transactions can be both voluntary or involuntary and are generally motivated either by the altruism of the donor of the malevolence of the recipient.

Exam Probability: **High**

44. *Answer choices:*

(see index for correct answer)

- a. Post-war consensus
- b. Social protection
- c. Poverty pimp
- d. Transfer payment

Guidance: level 1

:: Business cycle ::

In economics, the _____ is the reduction in the volatility of business cycle fluctuations in developed nations starting in the mid-1980s, compared with the decades before. It is believed to be caused by institutional and structural changes, particularly in central bank policies, in the later half of the twentieth century.

Exam Probability: **High**

45. *Answer choices:*

(see index for correct answer)

- a. Lundberg lag
- b. Great Moderation
- c. Business cycle
- d. Trough

Guidance: level 1

:: Numismatics ::

_____ is a currency without intrinsic value that has been established as money, often by government regulation. _____ does not have use value, and has value only because a government maintains its value, or because parties engaging in exchange agree on its value. It was introduced as an alternative to commodity money and representative money. Commodity money is created from a good, often a precious metal such as gold or silver, which has uses other than as a medium of exchange . Representative money is similar to _____ , but it represents a claim on a commodity .

46. *Answer choices:*

(see index for correct answer)

- a. First Strike Coins
- b. William Leslie Bowles
- c. Fiat money
- d. Anna Willess Williams

Guidance: level 1

:: Microeconomics ::

In microeconomics, the _____ states that, "conditional on all else being equal, as the price of a good increases , quantity demanded decreases ; conversely, as the price of a good decreases , quantity demanded ". In other words, the _____ describes an inverse relationship between price and quantity demanded of a good. Alternatively, other things being constant, quantity demanded of a commodity is inversely related to the price of the commodity. For example, a consumer may demand 2 kilograms of apples at $70 per kg; he may, however, demand 1 kg if the price rises to $80 per kg. This has been the general human behaviour on relationship between the price of the commodity and the quantity demanded. The factors held constant refer to other determinants of demand, such as the prices of other goods and the consumer's income. There are, however, some possible exceptions to the _____ , such as Giffen goods and Veblen goods.

47. *Answer choices:*

- a. Factors of production
- b. Minimum efficient scale
- c. Value
- d. Consumer surplus for software products

Guidance: level 1

:: Macroeconomic policy ::

In macroeconomics, _____ s are features of the structure of modern government budgets, particularly income taxes and welfare spending, that act to dampen fluctuations in real GDP.

Exam Probability: **High**

48. *Answer choices:*

- a. Automatic stabilizer
- b. Stabilization policy
- c. Policy-ineffectiveness proposition
- d. Automatic stabilizers

Guidance: level 1

:: Economics terminology ::

A _____ is a durable good that is used in the production of goods or services. _____ s are one of the three types of producer goods, the other two being land and labour. The three are also known collectively as "primary factors of production"

Exam Probability: **Low**

49. *Answer choices:*

(see index for correct answer)

- a. Capital good
- b. Technostructure
- c. equation of exchange
- d. Upside beta

Guidance: level 1

:: Fixed income market ::

The _____ is a financial market where participants can issue new debt, known as the primary market, or buy and sell debt securities, known as the secondary market. This is usually in the form of bonds, but it may include notes, bills, and so on.

50. *Answer choices:*

(see index for correct answer)

- a. Bond market
- b. Fixed deposit
- c. Fixed-income attribution
- d. Fixed income

Guidance: level 1

:: Policy ::

A _____ is a deliberate system of principles to guide decisions and achieve rational outcomes. A _____ is a statement of intent, and is implemented as a procedure or protocol. Policies are generally adopted by a governance body within an organization. Policies can assist in both subjective and objective decision making. Policies to assist in subjective decision making usually assist senior management with decisions that must be based on the relative merits of a number of factors, and as a result are often hard to test objectively, e.g. work-life balance _____ . In contrast policies to assist in objective decision making are usually operational in nature and can be objectively tested, e.g. password _____ .

51. *Answer choices:*

(see index for correct answer)

- a. Policy alienation
- b. Multifunctionality in agriculture
- c. Policy Monitoring
- d. Policy

Guidance: level 1

:: Property law ::

_____ is a legal designation for the ownership of property by non-governmental legal entities. _____ is distinguishable from public property, which is owned by a state entity; and from collective property, which is owned by a group of non-governmental entities. _____ can be either personal property or capital goods. _____ is a legal concept defined and enforced by a country's political system.

Exam Probability: **Medium**

52. *Answer choices:*
(see index for correct answer)

- a. Alienated land
- b. Numerus clausus
- c. Private property
- d. Finders, keepers

Guidance: level 1

:: United States housing bubble ::

In economics, a _____ is a business cycle contraction when there is a general decline in economic activity. Macroeconomic indicators such as GDP , investment spending, capacity utilization, household income, business profits, and inflation fall, while bankruptcies and the unemployment rate rise. In the United Kingdom, it is defined as a negative economic growth for two consecutive quarters.

Exam Probability: **High**

53. *Answer choices:*

(see index for correct answer)

- a. Cuyahoga Land Bank
- b. Shadow banking system
- c. subprime
- d. Speculative fever

Guidance: level 1

:: Banking ::

A _____ or term deposit is an interest-bearing bank deposit with a specified period of maturity. It is a money deposit at a banking institution that cannot be withdrawn for a specific term or period of time . When the term is over, it can be either withdrawn or held for another term. Generally speaking, the longer the term, the better the yield on the money.

54. *Answer choices:*

(see index for correct answer)

- a. monetary base
- b. Time deposit
- c. Anonymous Internet banking
- d. Coin roll hunting

Guidance: level 1

:: Macroeconomics ::

In economics, _____ is a hypothesized process by which people form their expectations about what will happen in the future based on what has happened in the past. For example, if inflation has been higher than expected in the past, people would revise expectations for the future.

Exam Probability: **Medium**

55. *Answer choices:*

(see index for correct answer)

- a. foreign investment
- b. Adaptive expectations
- c. Overheating

- d. Accounting reform

Guidance: level 1

:: Taxation ::

An _____ is a tax imposed on individuals or entities that varies with respective income or profits . _____ generally is computed as the product of a tax rate times taxable income. Taxation rates may vary by type or characteristics of the taxpayer.

Exam Probability: **Medium**

56. *Answer choices:*

(see index for correct answer)

- a. Backup withholding
- b. Stamp duty
- c. Directorate-General for Taxation and Customs Union
- d. Income tax

Guidance: level 1

:: Federal Reserve Banks ::

A _____ is a regional bank of the Federal Reserve System, the central banking system of the United States. There are twelve in total, one for each of the twelve Federal Reserve Districts that were created by the Federal Reserve Act of 1913. The banks are jointly responsible for implementing the monetary policy set forth by the Federal Open Market Committee, and are divided as follows.

Exam Probability: **High**

57. *Answer choices:*

(see index for correct answer)

- a. Federal Reserve Bank of Chicago
- b. Federal Reserve Bank
- c. Federal Reserve Bank of San Francisco, Los Angeles Branch
- d. Federal Reserve Bank of Boston

Guidance: level 1

:: Income distribution ::

In economics, _____ is how a nation's total GDP is distributed amongst its population. Income and its distribution have always been a central concern of economic theory and economic policy. Classical economists such as Adam Smith, Thomas Malthus, and David Ricardo were mainly concerned with factor _____ , that is, the distribution of income between the main factors of production, land, labour and capital. Modern economists have also addressed this issue, but have been more concerned with the distribution of income across individuals and households. Important theoretical and policy concerns include the balance between income inequality and economic growth, and their often inverse relationship.

Exam Probability: **Medium**

58. *Answer choices:*

(see index for correct answer)

- a. Factor income
- b. Guaranteed minimum income
- c. Redistributive justice
- d. The rich get richer and the poor get poorer

Guidance: level 1

:: Business cycle ::

An _____ is the phase of the business cycle following a recession, during which an economy regains and exceeds peak employment and output levels achieved prior to downturn. A recovery period is typically characterized by abnormally high levels of growth in real gross domestic product, employment, corporate profits, and other indicators.

Exam Probability: **Low**

59. *Answer choices:*

(see index for correct answer)

- a. Soft landing
- b. Economic recovery
- c. Lundberg lag
- d. Trough

Guidance: level 1

Business economics

Business economics is a field in applied economics which uses economic theory and quantitative methods to analyze business enterprises and the factors contributing to the diversity of organizational structures and the relationships of firms with labour, capital and product markets.

:: Industrial organization ::

In economics, specifically general equilibrium theory, a perfect market is defined by several idealizing conditions, collectively called _____ . In theoretical models where conditions of _____ hold, it has been theoretically demonstrated that a market will reach an equilibrium in which the quantity supplied for every product or service, including labor, equals the quantity demanded at the current price. This equilibrium would be a Pareto optimum.

Exam Probability: **Low**

1. *Answer choices:*

(see index for correct answer)

- a. American system of manufacturing
- b. Worldwide Responsible Accredited Production
- c. Path dependence
- d. Perfect competition

Guidance: level 1

:: Economics curves ::

In finance, the _____ is a curve showing several yields or interest rates across different contract lengths for a similar debt contract. The curve shows the relation between the interest rate and the time to maturity, known as the "term", of the debt for a given borrower in a given currency. For example, the U.S. dollar interest rates paid on U.S. Treasury securities for various maturities are closely watched by many traders, and are commonly plotted on a graph such as the one on the right which is informally called "the _____ ". More formal mathematical descriptions of this relation are often called the term structure of interest rates.

Exam Probability: **High**

2. *Answer choices:*

- a. Yield curve
- b. Marginal propensity to save
- c. Engel curve
- d. Kuznets curve

Guidance: level 1

:: Microeconomics ::

In economics and related disciplines, a _____ is a cost in making any economic trade when participating in a market.

Exam Probability: **Medium**

3. *Answer choices:*

(see index for correct answer)

- a. Feasibility condition
- b. Bliss point
- c. Total cost
- d. False economy

Guidance: level 1

:: Subprime mortgage crisis ::

_____ , Inc., abbreviated to WaMu, was a savings bank holding company and the former owner of _____ Bank, which was the United States' largest savings and loan association until its collapse in 2008.

Exam Probability: **High**

4. *Answer choices:*

(see index for correct answer)

- a. Subprime mortgage crisis
- b. Foreclosure rescue
- c. Foreclosure rescue scheme
- d. Washington Mutual

Guidance: level 1

:: Corporate finance ::

_____ , in the global financial market, is an unsecured promissory note with a fixed maturity of not more than 270 days.

Exam Probability: **High**

5. *Answer choices:*

(see index for correct answer)

- a. Stakeholder theory
- b. Buyout
- c. Treasury stock
- d. Bond Tender Offer

Guidance: level 1

:: Probability distributions ::

In probability theory and statistics, a _____ is a mathematical function that provides the probabilities of occurrence of different possible outcomes in an experiment. In more technical terms, the _____ is a description of a random phenomenon in terms of the probabilities of events. For instance, if the random variable X is used to denote the outcome of a coin toss , then the _____ of X would take the value 0.5 for X = heads, and 0.5 for X = tails . Examples of random phenomena can include the results of an experiment or survey.

Exam Probability: **Low**

6. *Answer choices:*

(see index for correct answer)

- a. Nakagami distribution
- b. Slash distribution
- c. Generalized multivariate log-gamma distribution
- d. Probability distribution

Guidance: level 1

:: Insurance ::

_____ is a form of health insurance designed to pay a portion of the costs associated with dental care. There are several different types of individual, family, or group _____ plans grouped into three primary categories: Indemnity, Preferred Provider Network , and Dental Health Managed Organizations .

7. *Answer choices:*

- a. Home insurance
- b. Premium Financing
- c. Margin on services
- d. Dental insurance

Guidance: level 1

:: Derivatives (finance) ::

In options trading, a _____ is a bearish, vertical spread options strategy that can be used when the options trader is moderately bearish on the underlying security.

Exam Probability: **Low**

8. *Answer choices:*

- a. Constant proportion debt obligation
- b. Area yield options contract
- c. Conditional variance swap
- d. Bear spread

:: Scarcity ::

In economics, _____ is any payment to an owner or factor of production in excess of the costs needed to bring that factor into production. In classical economics, _____ is any payment made or benefit received for non-produced inputs such as location and for assets formed by creating official privilege over natural opportunities . In the moral economy of neoclassical economics, _____ includes income gained by labor or state beneficiaries of other "contrived" exclusivity, such as labor guilds and unofficial corruption.

Exam Probability: **Low**

9. *Answer choices:*

(see index for correct answer)

- a. Economic rent
- b. Artificial scarcity
- c. Excess demand
- d. Post-Scarcity Anarchism

:: Financial economics ::

_____ is a term related to the inter-party relationships of a transaction. It is usually defined as the extent to which the investments made to support a particular transaction have a higher value to that transaction than they would have if they were redeployed for any other purpose. _____ has been extensively studied in a variety of management and economics areas such as marketing, accounting, organizational behavior and management information systems.

Exam Probability: **Medium**

10. *Answer choices:*

(see index for correct answer)

- a. Added value
- b. Asset specificity
- c. Financial Literacy and Education Commission
- d. Business value

Guidance: level 1

:: Elasticity (economics) ::

In mathematics and economics, the _____ is the elasticity of one variable with respect to another between two given points. It is the ratio of the percentage change of one of the variables between the two points to the percentage change of the other variable. It contrasts with the point elasticity, which is the limit of the _____ as the distance between the two points approaches zero and which hence is defined at a single point rather than for a pair of points.

11. *Answer choices:*

(see index for correct answer)

- a. Arc elasticity
- b. Output elasticity
- c. Price elasticity of supply
- d. Cross elasticity of demand

Guidance: level 1

:: Commerce ::

In trade, _____ is a system of exchange where participants in a transaction directly exchange goods or services for other goods or services without using a medium of exchange, such as money. Economists distinguish _____ from gift economies in many ways; _____ , for example, features immediate reciprocal exchange, not delayed in time. _____ usually takes place on a bilateral basis, but may be multilateral . In most developed countries, _____ usually only exists parallel to monetary systems to a very limited extent. Market actors use _____ as a replacement for money as the method of exchange in times of monetary crisis, such as when currency becomes unstable or simply unavailable for conducting commerce.

12. *Answer choices:*

(see index for correct answer)

- a. Sell-side analyst
- b. Barter
- c. Linestanding
- d. Haul video

Guidance: level 1

:: Global systemically important banks ::

_____ Inc. or Citi is an American multinational investment bank and financial services corporation headquartered in New York City. The company was formed by the merger of banking giant Citicorp and financial conglomerate Travelers Group in 1998; Travelers was subsequently spun off from the company in 2002. _____ owns Citicorp, the holding company for Citibank, as well as several international subsidiaries.

Exam Probability: **High**

13. *Answer choices:*
(see index for correct answer)

- a. Groupe BPCE
- b. Wells Fargo
- c. Barclays
- d. Citigroup

Guidance: level 1

:: International economics ::

In modern monetary policy, a _____ is an official lowering of the value of a country's currency within a fixed exchange rate system, by which the monetary authority formally sets a new fixed rate with respect to a foreign reference currency or currency basket. In contrast, a depreciation is a decrease in a currency's value due to market forces under a floating exchange rate, not government or central bank policy actions.

Exam Probability: **Low**

14. *Answer choices:*

(see index for correct answer)

- a. Spaghetti bowl effect
- b. Devaluation
- c. Sterilization
- d. International economics

Guidance: level 1

:: Systemic risk ::

_____ Holdings Inc. was a global financial services firm. Before filing for bankruptcy in 2008, Lehman was the fourth-largest investment bank in the United States , doing business in investment banking, equity and fixed-income sales and trading , research, investment management, private equity, and private banking. Lehman was operational for 158 years from its founding in 1850 until 2008.

Exam Probability: **Medium**

15. *Answer choices:*

(see index for correct answer)

- a. Clearing house
- b. Lehman Brothers
- c. Procyclical and countercyclical
- d. Swap Execution Facility

Guidance: level 1

:: Rationing and licensing ::

_____ is the controlled distribution of scarce resources, goods, services, or an artificial restriction of demand. _____ controls the size of the ration, which is one's allowed portion of the resources being distributed on a particular day or at a particular time. There are many forms of _____ , and in western civilization people experience some of them in daily life without realizing it.

16. *Answer choices:*

(see index for correct answer)

- a. First-come, first-served
- b. Rationing
- c. Road space rationing in Beijing
- d. CC41

Guidance: level 1

:: Trade policy ::

_____ is a trade policy that does not restrict imports or exports; it can also be understood as the free market idea applied to international trade. In government, _____ is predominantly advocated by political parties that hold liberal economic positions while economically left-wing and nationalist political parties generally support protectionism, the opposite of _____ .

Exam Probability: **Medium**

17. *Answer choices:*

(see index for correct answer)

- a. Free trade
- b. Green box policies

- c. Free trade zone
- d. Commercial policy

Guidance: level 1

:: Financial risk ::

_____ is concerned with financial policies regarding paying cash dividend in the present or paying an increased dividend at a later stage. Whether to issue dividends, and what amount, is determined mainly on the basis of the company's unappropriated profit and influenced by the company's long-term earning power. When cash surplus exists and is not needed by the firm, then management is expected to pay out some or all of those surplus earnings in the form of cash dividends or to repurchase the company's stock through a share buyback program.

Exam Probability: **Low**

18. *Answer choices:*

(see index for correct answer)

- a. Settlement risk
- b. Operational risk
- c. Dividend policy
- d. Financial Stability Board

Guidance: level 1

:: Private equity ::

A _____ is a financial transaction in which a company is purchased with a combination of equity and debt, such that the company's cash flow is the collateral used to secure and repay the borrowed money. The use of debt, which normally has a lower cost of capital than equity, serves to reduce the overall cost of financing the acquisition. The cost of debt is lower because interest payments often reduce corporate income tax liability, whereas dividend payments normally do not. This reduced cost of financing allows greater gains to accrue to the equity, and, as a result, the debt serves as a lever to increase the returns to the equity.

Exam Probability: **Low**

19. *Answer choices:*

(see index for correct answer)

- a. Management fee
- b. Pre-money valuation
- c. Pledge fund
- d. Angel investor

Guidance: level 1

:: Financial terminology ::

_____ typically refers to investment funds, generally organized as limited partnerships, that buy and restructure companies that are not publicly traded.

Exam Probability: **High**

20. *Answer choices:*

(see index for correct answer)

- a. Capital structure substitution theory
- b. Cost price
- c. EBDIT
- d. Private equity

Guidance: level 1

:: Microeconomics ::

In economics, _____ is the change in the total cost that arises when the quantity produced is incremented by one unit; that is, it is the cost of producing one more unit of a good. Intuitively, _____ at each level of production includes the cost of any additional inputs required to produce the next unit. At each level of production and time period being considered, _____ s include all costs that vary with the level of production, whereas other costs that do not vary with production are fixed and thus have no _____ . For example, the _____ of producing an automobile will generally include the costs of labor and parts needed for the additional automobile but not the fixed costs of the factory that have already been incurred. In practice, marginal analysis is segregated into short and long-run cases, so that, over the long run, all costs become marginal. Where there are economies of scale, prices set at _____ will fail to cover total costs, thus requiring a subsidy. _____ pricing is not a matter of merely lowering the general level of prices with the aid of a subsidy; with or without subsidy it calls for a drastic restructuring of pricing practices, with opportunities for very substantial improvements in efficiency at critical points.

Exam Probability: **High**

21. *Answer choices:*

(see index for correct answer)

- a. Surface Freight Forwarder Deregulation Act of 1986
- b. Marginal cost
- c. inelastic
- d. Incentive

Guidance: level 1

:: Financial markets ::

A _____ is a market in which people trade financial securities and derivatives such as futures and options at low transaction costs. Securities include stocks and bonds, and precious metals.

Exam Probability: **Medium**

22. *Answer choices:*

(see index for correct answer)

- a. Financial instrument
- b. Primary Dealer Credit Facility
- c. Price limit
- d. Financial market

Guidance: level 1

:: International taxation ::

In taxation and accounting, _____ refers to the rules and methods for pricing transactions within and between enterprises under common ownership or control. Because of the potential for cross-border controlled transactions to distort taxable income, tax authorities in many countries can adjust intragroup transfer prices that differ from what would have been charged by unrelated enterprises dealing at arm's length . The OECD and World Bank recommend intragroup pricing rules based on the arm's-length principle, and 19 of the 20 members of the G20 have adopted similar measures through bilateral treaties and domestic legislation, regulations, or administrative practice. Countries with _____ legislation generally follow the OECD _____ Guidelines for Multinational Enterprises and Tax Administrations in most respects, although their rules can differ on some important details.

Exam Probability: **Medium**

23. *Answer choices:*

(see index for correct answer)

- a. Transfer pricing
- b. Spahn tax
- c. Foreign earned income exclusion
- d. Euromod

Guidance: level 1

:: Investment ::

In finance, the _____ or net present worth applies to a series of cash flows occurring at different times. The present value of a cash flow depends on the interval of time between now and the cash flow. It also depends on the discount rate. NPV accounts for the time value of money. It provides a method for evaluating and comparing capital projects or financial products with cash flows spread over time, as in loans, investments, payouts from insurance contracts plus many other applications.

Exam Probability: Medium

24. *Answer choices:*

(see index for correct answer)

- a. LLCR
- b. Loan officer
- c. Displaced sales
- d. Net present value

Guidance: level 1

:: Financial markets ::

In finance, the _____ is a model used to determine a theoretically appropriate required rate of return of an asset, to make decisions about adding assets to a well-diversified portfolio.

Exam Probability: High

25. *Answer choices:*

(see index for correct answer)

- a. Alternext
- b. Capital asset pricing model
- c. Block trade
- d. Issuer

Guidance: level 1

:: Investment ::

_____ , and investment appraisal, is the planning process used to determine whether an organization`s long term investments such as new machinery, replacement of machinery, new plants, new products, and research development projects are worth the funding of cash through the firm`s capitalization structure . It is the process of allocating resources for major capital, or investment, expenditures. One of the primary goals of _____ investments is to increase the value of the firm to the shareholders.

Exam Probability: **Medium**

26. *Answer choices:*

(see index for correct answer)

- a. Search fund
- b. Displaced sales
- c. Tail risk parity

- d. Widow-and-orphan stock

Guidance: level 1

:: Microeconomics ::

A _____ is the price of a commodity such as a good or service in terms of another; i.e., the ratio of two prices. A _____ may be expressed in terms of a ratio between the prices of any two goods or the ratio between the price of one good and the price of a market basket of goods . A _____ is an opportunity cost. Microeconomics can be seen as the study of how economic agents react to changes in _____ s, and of how _____ s are affected by the behavior of those agents.

Exam Probability: **Medium**

27. *Answer choices:*
(see index for correct answer)

- a. Relative price
- b. Search cost
- c. Yield management
- d. RevPAR

Guidance: level 1

:: Market structure and pricing ::

_____ is the percentage of a market accounted for by a specific entity. In a survey of nearly 200 senior marketing managers, 67% responded that they found the revenue- "dollar _____" metric very useful, while 61% found "unit _____" very useful.

Exam Probability: Low

28. *Answer choices:*

(see index for correct answer)

- a. Open source
- b. Megacorpstate
- c. Socially optimal firm size
- d. Pricing strategies

Guidance: level 1

:: Business economics ::

In economics, _____ is demand for a factor of production or intermediate good that occurs as a result of the demand for another intermediate or final good. In essence, the demand for, say, a factor of production by a firm is dependent on the demand by consumers for the product produced by the firm. The term was first introduced by Alfred Marshall in his Principles of Economics in 1890.

Exam Probability: Medium

29. *Answer choices:*

(see index for correct answer)

- a. Overnight cost
- b. Consumer economy
- c. Derived demand
- d. Units of transportation measurement

Guidance: level 1

:: Energy economics ::

The Organization of the Petroleum Exporting Countries is an intergovernmental organization of 14 nations, founded in 1960 in Baghdad by the first five members , and headquartered since 1965 in Vienna, Austria. As of September 2018, the then 14 member countries accounted for an estimated 44 percent of global oil production and 81.5 percent of the world's "proven" oil reserves, giving _____ a major influence on global oil prices that were previously determined by the so called "Seven Sisters" grouping of multinational oil companies.

Exam Probability: **Low**

30. *Answer choices:*

(see index for correct answer)

- a. Clean coal technology
- b. Dynamic demand

- c. Differential tariff
- d. Directive on the energy performance of buildings

Guidance: level 1

:: Derivatives (finance) ::

In options trading, a _____ is a bullish, vertical spread options strategy that is designed to profit from a moderate rise in the price of the underlying security.

Exam Probability: **Medium**

31. *Answer choices:*

(see index for correct answer)

- a. Bull spread
- b. Foreign exchange swap
- c. Risk-neutral measure
- d. Exchange-traded derivative contract

Guidance: level 1

:: Financial ratios ::

_____ is a measure of how revenue growth translates into growth in operating income. It is a measure of leverage, and of how risky, or volatile, a company's operating income is.

Exam Probability: **Medium**

32. *Answer choices:*

(see index for correct answer)

- a. Operating leverage
- b. Debtor days
- c. Quick ratio
- d. Sales density

Guidance: level 1

:: Marketing ::

A _____ is the quantity of payment or compensation given by one party to another in return for one unit of goods or services.. A _____ is influenced by both production costs and demand for the product. A _____ may be determined by a monopolist or may be imposed on the firm by market conditions.

Exam Probability: **Medium**

33. *Answer choices:*

(see index for correct answer)

- a. Niche market
- b. Davie-Brown Index
- c. Demand chain
- d. All-commodity volume

Guidance: level 1

:: Economic indicators ::

The _____ describes the strength of a currency relative to a basket of other currencies. Although typically the basket is trade weighted, there are others besides the trade-weighted _____ .

Exam Probability: **Low**

34. *Answer choices:*

(see index for correct answer)

- a. Effective exchange rate index
- b. Keqiang index
- c. National Compensation Survey
- d. Penn World Table

Guidance: level 1

:: Commerce ::

_____ , Inc. is an American media-services provider headquartered in Los Gatos, California, founded in 1997 by Reed Hastings and Marc Randolph in Scotts Valley, California. The company's primary business is its subscription-based streaming OTT service which offers online streaming of a library of films and television programs, including those produced in-house. As of April 2019, _____ had over 148 million paid subscriptions worldwide, including 60 million in the United States, and over 154 million subscriptions total including free trials. It is available almost worldwide except in mainland China as well as Syria, North Korea, and Crimea . The company also has offices in the Netherlands, Brazil, India, Japan, and South Korea. _____ is a member of the Motion Picture Association of America .

Exam Probability: **Medium**

35. *Answer choices:*

(see index for correct answer)

- a. Requisition
- b. Bunker adjustment factor
- c. Straw purchase
- d. Netflix

Guidance: level 1

:: Market structure and pricing ::

_____ is any process whereby a state lifts restrictions on some private individual activities. _____ occurs when something which used to be banned is no longer banned, or when government regulations are relaxed.

36. *Answer choices:*

(see index for correct answer)

- a. Market share analysis
- b. industry concentration
- c. Market concentration
- d. Liberalization

Guidance: level 1

:: Goods ::

In economics, a _____ is a good that is both non-excludable and non-rivalrous in that individuals cannot be excluded from use or could be enjoyed without paying for it, and where use by one individual does not reduce availability to others or the goods can be effectively consumed simultaneously by more than one person. This is in contrast to a common good which is non-excludable but is rivalrous to a certain degree.

37. *Answer choices:*

(see index for correct answer)

- a. Demerit good
- b. Public good
- c. Case
- d. Anti-rival good

Guidance: level 1

:: Dividends ::

A _____ is a payment made by a corporation to its shareholders, usually as a distribution of profits. When a corporation earns a profit or surplus, the corporation is able to re-invest the profit in the business and pay a proportion of the profit as a _____ to shareholders. Distribution to shareholders may be in cash or, if the corporation has a _____ reinvestment plan, the amount can be paid by the issue of further shares or share repurchase. When _____ s are paid, shareholders typically must pay income taxes, and the corporation does not receive a corporate income tax deduction for the _____ payments.

Exam Probability: **Medium**

38. *Answer choices:*

(see index for correct answer)

- a. Dividend
- b. Dividend stripping

- c. Dividend cover
- d. East India Stock Dividend Redemption Act 1873

Guidance: level 1

:: Financial ratios ::

_____ is a financial ratio that indicates the percentage of a company's assets that are provided via debt. It is the ratio of total debt and total assets .

Exam Probability: **Low**

39. *Answer choices:*

(see index for correct answer)

- a. Gross margin
- b. Average accounting return
- c. Debt ratio
- d. Price/cash flow ratio

Guidance: level 1

:: Sales ::

The seller, or the provider of the goods or services, completes a sale in response to an acquisition, appropriation, requisition or a direct interaction with the buyer at the point of sale. There is a passing of title of the item, and the settlement of a price, in which agreement is reached on a price for which transfer of ownership of the item will occur. The seller, not the purchaser typically executes the sale and it may be completed prior to the obligation of payment. In the case of indirect interaction, a person who sells goods or service on behalf of the owner is known as a salesman or saleswoman or salesperson, but this often refers to someone _____ goods in a store/shop, in which case other terms are also common, including salesclerk, shop assistant, and retail clerk.

40. *Answer choices:*

(see index for correct answer)

- a. Presales
- b. Conditional sale
- c. Sale and rent back
- d. Vorsight

Guidance: level 1

:: Foreign direct investment ::

_____ is the levying of tax by two or more jurisdictions on the same declared income , asset , or financial transaction . Double liability is mitigated in a number of ways, for example.

41. *Answer choices:*

(see index for correct answer)

- a. Double taxation
- b. Trade and Investment Framework Agreement
- c. Permanent Court of Arbitration
- d. Expropriation

Guidance: level 1

:: History of banking ::

_____ was a British merchant bank based in London, and the world's second oldest merchant bank . It was founded in 1762 by Francis Baring, a British-born member of the German-British Baring family of merchants and bankers.

Exam Probability: **Medium**

42. *Answer choices:*

(see index for correct answer)

- a. Barings Bank
- b. 3-6-3 Rule
- c. Private equity in the 1990s

- d. Lombard banking

Guidance: level 1

:: Health economics ::

The _____ was an experimental study of health care costs, utilization and outcomes in the United States, which assigned people randomly to different kinds of plans and followed their behavior, from 1974 to 1982. Because it was a randomized controlled trial, it provided stronger evidence than the more common observational studies. It concluded that cost sharing reduced "inappropriate or unnecessary" medical care , but also reduced "appropriate or needed" medical care.

Exam Probability: **High**

43. *Answer choices:*

(see index for correct answer)

- a. Medical Banking
- b. Fee splitting
- c. Health care reform debate in the United States
- d. RAND Health Insurance Experiment

Guidance: level 1

:: Financial ratios ::

The _____ shows the percentage of how profitable a company's assets are in generating revenue.

Exam Probability: **Low**

44. *Answer choices:*
(see index for correct answer)

- a. Debt-to-capital ratio
- b. Bias ratio
- c. Retention rate
- d. Equity ratio

Guidance: level 1

:: Promotion and marketing communications ::

_____ is a marketing communication that employs an openly sponsored, non-personal message to promote or sell a product, service or idea. Sponsors of _____ are typically businesses wishing to promote their products or services. _____ is differentiated from public relations in that an advertiser pays for and has control over the message. It differs from personal selling in that the message is non-personal, i.e., not directed to a particular individual. _____ is communicated through various mass media, including traditional media such as newspapers, magazines, television, radio, outdoor _____ or direct mail; and new media such as search results, blogs, social media, websites or text messages. The actual presentation of the message in a medium is referred to as an advertisement, or "ad" or advert for short.

45. *Answer choices:*

(see index for correct answer)

- a. World Perfume
- b. Database marketing
- c. Social marketing intelligence
- d. Advertising

Guidance: level 1

:: Stock market ::

A _____ , securities exchange or bourse, is a facility where stock
brokers and traders can buy and sell securities, such as shares of stock and
bonds and other financial instruments. _____ s may also provide for
facilities the issue and redemption of such securities and instruments and
capital events including the payment of income and dividends. Securities traded
on a _____ include stock issued by listed companies, unit trusts,
derivatives, pooled investment products and bonds. _____ s often function
as "continuous auction" markets with buyers and sellers consummating
transactions via open outcry at a central location such as the floor of the
exchange or by using an electronic trading platform.

Exam Probability: **Medium**

46. *Answer choices:*

(see index for correct answer)

- a. Security
- b. Options broker
- c. Red herring prospectus
- d. Stock exchange

Guidance: level 1

:: Financial ratios ::

_____ or asset turns is a financial ratio that measures the efficiency of a company's use of its assets in generating sales revenue or sales income to the company.

Exam Probability: **Medium**

47. *Answer choices:*

(see index for correct answer)

- a. Asset turnover
- b. Accounting liquidity
- c. Sustainable growth rate
- d. Social return on investment

Guidance: level 1

:: Microeconomics ::

In financial accounting, an _____ is any resource owned by the business. Anything tangible or intangible that can be owned or controlled to produce value and that is held by a company to produce positive economic value is an _____ . Simply stated, _____ s represent value of ownership that can be converted into cash . The balance sheet of a firm records the monetary value of the _____ s owned by that firm. It covers money and other valuables belonging to an individual or to a business.

Exam Probability: **Medium**

48. *Answer choices:*

(see index for correct answer)

- a. Missing market
- b. Tax choice
- c. Value
- d. Asset

Guidance: level 1

:: Financial risk ::

The _____ on a financial investment is the expected value of its return . It is a measure of the center of the distribution of the random variable that is the return.

Exam Probability: **Low**

(see index for correct answer)

49. *Answer choices:*

- a. Reputational risk
- b. Liquidity risk
- c. Political risk
- d. Expected return

Guidance: level 1

:: Auditing ::

_____ refers to the independence of the internal auditor or of the external auditor from parties that may have a financial interest in the business being audited. Independence requires integrity and an objective approach to the audit process. The concept requires the auditor to carry out his or her work freely and in an objective manner.

Exam Probability: **Medium**

50. *Answer choices:*

(see index for correct answer)

- a. Communication audit
- b. Chartered Institute of Internal Auditors
- c. Legal auditing
- d. Auditor independence

:: Sampling (statistics) ::

_____ is the information received by means of the senses, particularly by observation and documentation of patterns and behavior through experimentation. The term comes from the Greek word for experience, μπεα .

Exam Probability: **Low**

51. *Answer choices:*

- a. Sampling frame
- b. survey data
- c. sample size
- d. Acceptance sampling

:: Financial crises ::

A _____ occurs when a large number of people withdraw their money from a bank, because they believe the bank may cease to function in the near future. In other words, it is when, in a fractional-reserve banking system , a large number of customers withdraw cash from deposit accounts with a financial institution at the same time because they believe that the financial institution is, or might become, insolvent; they keep the cash or transfer it into other assets, such as government bonds, precious metals or gemstones. When they transfer funds to another institution, it may be characterized as a capital flight. As a _____ progresses, it generates its own momentum: as more people withdraw cash, the likelihood of default increases, triggering further withdrawals. This can destabilize the bank to the point where it runs out of cash and thus faces sudden bankruptcy. To combat a _____ , a bank may limit how much cash each customer may withdraw, suspend withdrawals altogether, or promptly acquire more cash from other banks or from the central bank, besides other measures.

Exam Probability: **Low**

52. *Answer choices:*

(see index for correct answer)

- a. Credit crisis of 1772
- b. Panic of 1825
- c. Bank run
- d. 2010 United States foreclosure crisis

Guidance: level 1

:: Investment ::

The _____ is a measure of an investment's rate of return. The term internal refers to the fact that the calculation excludes external factors, such as the risk-free rate, inflation, the cost of capital, or various financial risks.

Exam Probability: **High**

53. *Answer choices:*

(see index for correct answer)

- a. Performance attribution
- b. Intellidex
- c. Internal rate of return
- d. Greater fool theory

Guidance: level 1

:: Health economics ::

_____ is a form of economic analysis that compares the relative costs and outcomes of different courses of action. _____ is distinct from cost–benefit analysis, which assigns a monetary value to the measure of effect. _____ is often used in the field of health services, where it may be inappropriate to monetize health effect. Typically the CEA is expressed in terms of a ratio where the denominator is a gain in health from a measure and the numerator is the cost associated with the health gain. The most commonly used outcome measure is quality-adjusted life years .

54. *Answer choices:*

(see index for correct answer)

- a. Cost-effectiveness analysis
- b. Fee splitting
- c. Comparative effectiveness research
- d. Oregon Medicaid health experiment

Guidance: level 1

:: Financial markets ::

For an individual, a _____ is the minimum amount of money by which the expected return on a risky asset must exceed the known return on a risk-free asset in order to induce an individual to hold the risky asset rather than the risk-free asset. It is positive if the person is risk averse. Thus it is the minimum willingness to accept compensation for the risk.

Exam Probability: **High**

55. *Answer choices:*

(see index for correct answer)

- a. Form 3
- b. Flight-to-liquidity

- c. Risk premium
- d. MetaTrader 4

Guidance: level 1

:: Capitalism ::

_____ or globalisation is the process of interaction and integration among people, companies, and governments worldwide. As a complex and multifaceted phenomenon, _____ is considered by some as a form of capitalist expansion which entails the integration of local and national economies into a global, unregulated market economy. _____ has grown due to advances in transportation and communication technology. With the increased global interactions comes the growth of international trade, ideas, and culture. _____ is primarily an economic process of interaction and integration that's associated with social and cultural aspects. However, conflicts and diplomacy are also large parts of the history of _____ , and modern _____ .

Exam Probability: **Low**

56. *Answer choices:*

(see index for correct answer)

- a. mixed economies
- b. Globalization
- c. Gentlemanly capitalism
- d. Positive non-interventionism

:: Financial markets ::

In economics, _____ is the process by which, in an economic market, the supply of whatever is traded is equated to the demand, so that there is no leftover supply or demand. The new classical economics assumes that, in any given market, assuming that all buyers and sellers have access to information and that there is not "friction" impeding price changes, prices always adjust up or down to ensure _____ .

Exam Probability: **High**

57. *Answer choices:*

(see index for correct answer)

- a. Real prices and ideal prices
- b. Market clearing
- c. High-frequency trading
- d. Copy trading

:: Marketing ::

A _____ is something that is necessary for an organism to live a healthy life. _____ s are distinguished from wants in that, in the case of a _____ , a deficiency causes a clear adverse outcome: a dysfunction or death. In other words, a _____ is something required for a safe, stable and healthy life while a want is a desire, wish or aspiration. When _____ s or wants are backed by purchasing power, they have the potential to become economic demands.

Exam Probability: **Low**

58. *Answer choices:*

(see index for correct answer)

- a. Interactive marketing
- b. Need
- c. Notability
- d. Pitching engine

Guidance: level 1

:: Asymmetric information ::

In economics, _____ occurs when someone increases their exposure to risk when insured, especially when a person takes more risks because someone else bears the cost of those risks. A _____ may occur where the actions of one party may change to the detriment of another after a financial transaction has taken place.

59. *Answer choices:*

(see index for correct answer)

- a. Principal
- b. Adverse selection
- c. Moral hazard
- d. Credence good

Guidance: level 1

International economics

International economics is concerned with the effects upon economic activity from international differences in productive resources and consumer preferences and the international institutions that affect them. It seeks to explain the patterns and consequences of transactions and interactions between the inhabitants of different countries, including trade, investment and migration.

:: History of banking ::

A _____ is a monetary system in which the standard economic unit of account is based on a fixed quantity of gold. Three types can be distinguished: specie, bullion, and exchange.

1. *Answer choices:*

(see index for correct answer)

- a. Stadsleenbank Delft
- b. Barings Bank
- c. Gold standard
- d. Goldschmidt family

Guidance: level 1

:: Developing 8 Countries member states ::

_____ , officially the Republic of _____ , is a country in Southeast Asia, between the Indian and Pacific oceans. It is the world's largest island country, with more than seventeen thousand islands, and at 1,904,569 square kilometres , the 14th largest by land area and the 7th largest in combined sea and land area. With over 261 million people, it is the world's 4th most populous country as well as the most populous Muslim-majority country. Java, the world's most populous island, is home to more than half of the country's population.

2. *Answer choices:*

(see index for correct answer)

- a. Malaysia
- b. Pakistan
- c. Nigeria
- d. Egypt

Guidance: level 1

:: International trade ::

_____ is the process of a company increasing production of goods or services at the same part of the supply chain. A company may do this via internal expansion, acquisition or merger.

Exam Probability: **High**

3. *Answer choices:*

(see index for correct answer)

- a. International commercial law
- b. SinoLatin Capital
- c. International Organisation of Employers
- d. Horizontal integration

Guidance: level 1

:: International trade ::

_____ , also known as anti-subsidy duties, are trade import duties imposed under World Trade Organization rules to neutralize the negative effects of subsidies. They are imposed after an investigation finds that a foreign country subsidizes its exports, injuring domestic producers in the importing country. According to World Trade Organization rules, a country can launch its own investigation and decide to charge extra duties, provided such additional duties are in accordance with the GATT Article VI and the GATT Agreement on Subsidies and Countervailing Measures.

Exam Probability: **High**

4. *Answer choices:*

(see index for correct answer)

- a. Trade office
- b. Country commercial guides
- c. Social dumping
- d. TradeCard

Guidance: level 1

:: Financial markets ::

The _____ is the informal over-the-counter financial market by which contracts for future delivery are entered into. Standardized forward contracts are called futures contracts and traded on a futures exchange.

Exam Probability: **Low**

5. *Answer choices:*

(see index for correct answer)

- a. Market sector
- b. Forward market
- c. Committee on Capital Markets Regulation
- d. Alternative trading system

Guidance: level 1

:: Economic integration ::

A free-trade area is the region encompassing a trade bloc whose member countries have signed a free trade agreement . Such agreements involve cooperation between at least two countries to reduce trade barriers import quotas and tariffs and to increase trade of goods and services with each other.If people are also free to move between the countries, in addition to a free-trade agreement, it would also be considered an open border. It can be considered the second stage of economic integration.

Exam Probability: **Medium**

6. *Answer choices:*

(see index for correct answer)

- a. Customs territory
- b. Complete economic integration
- c. Levant Union
- d. North American integration

Guidance: level 1

:: International economics ::

_____ is the characteristic of self-sufficiency; the term usually applies to political states or to their economic systems. _____ exists whenever an entity can survive or continue its activities without external assistance or international trade. If a self-sufficient economy also refuses all trade with the outside world then economists may term it a closed economy. The term "closed economy" is also used technically as an abstraction to allow consideration of a single economy without taking foreign trade into account – i.e. as the antonym of "open economy". _____ in the political sense is not necessarily an economic phenomenon; for example, a military _____ would be a state that could defend itself without help from another country, or could manufacture all of its weapons without any imports from the outside world.

Exam Probability: **Low**

7. *Answer choices:*

(see index for correct answer)

- a. Devaluation
- b. Sudden stop
- c. Multinational corporation
- d. Rybczynski theorem

Guidance: level 1

:: Energy economics ::

The Organization of the Petroleum Exporting Countries is an intergovernmental organization of 14 nations, founded in 1960 in Baghdad by the first five members , and headquartered since 1965 in Vienna, Austria. As of September 2018, the then 14 member countries accounted for an estimated 44 percent of global oil production and 81.5 percent of the world's "proven" oil reserves, giving _____ a major influence on global oil prices that were previously determined by the so called "Seven Sisters" grouping of multinational oil companies.

Exam Probability: **High**

8. *Answer choices:*

(see index for correct answer)

- a. Petrodollar warfare
- b. Directive on the energy performance of buildings
- c. OPEC
- d. Human Ecology, Human Economy

:: Petroleum economics ::

The _____ was a period when the major industrial countries of the world, particularly the United States, Canada, Western Europe, Japan, Australia, and New Zealand, faced substantial petroleum shortages, real and perceived, as well as elevated prices. The two worst crises of this period were the 1973 oil crisis and the 1979 energy crisis, when the Yom Kippur War and the Iranian Revolution triggered interruptions in Middle Eastern oil exports.

Exam Probability: **Low**

9. *Answer choices:*

(see index for correct answer)

- a. Formation evaluation
- b. Asymmetric price transmission
- c. Strategic petroleum reserve
- d. 1970s energy crisis

:: Foreign exchange market ::

The _____ is a multilateral currency swap arrangement among the ten members of the Association of Southeast Asian Nations , the People's Republic of China , Japan, and South Korea. It draws from a foreign exchange reserves pool worth US$120 billion and was launched on 24 March 2010. That pool has been expanded to $240 billion in 2012.

Exam Probability: **Low**

10. *Answer choices:*

(see index for correct answer)

- a. Chiang Mai Initiative
- b. Bowers v. Kerbaugh-Empire Co.
- c. Exorbitant privilege
- d. Triangular arbitrage

Guidance: level 1

:: Financial risk ::

All businesses take risks based on two factors: the probability an adverse circumstance will come about and the cost of such adverse circumstance.Risk management is the study of how to control risks and balance the possibility of gains.

Exam Probability: **Medium**

11. *Answer choices:*

(see index for correct answer)

- a. Risk-weighted asset
- b. Market risk
- c. Single loss expectancy
- d. Liquidity risk

Guidance: level 1

:: Taxation ::

In a tax system, the _____ is the ratio at which a business or person is taxed. There are several methods used to present a _____ : statutory, average, marginal, and effective. These rates can also be presented using different definitions applied to a tax base: inclusive and exclusive.

Exam Probability: **High**

12. *Answer choices:*

(see index for correct answer)

- a. Fiscal memory devices
- b. Tax exemption
- c. Tax rate
- d. Tax basis

:: Game theory ::

In economics, _____ theory attempts to explain the behavior of supply, demand, and prices in a whole economy with several or many interacting markets, by seeking to prove that the interaction of demand and supply will result in an overall _____ . _____ theory contrasts to the theory of partial equilibrium, which only analyzes single markets.

Exam Probability: **High**

13. *Answer choices:*

(see index for correct answer)

- a. Outcome
- b. Pirate game
- c. Coordination game
- d. Evolutionarily stable strategy

:: International economics ::

The _____ is a hypothesized concentration of certain industries in large markets. The _____ became part of New Trade Theory. Through trade theory, the _____ is derived from models with returns to scale and transportation costs. When it is cheaper for an industry to operate in a single country because of returns to scale, an industry will base itself in the country where most of its products are consumed in order to minimize transportation costs. The _____ implies a link between market size and exports that is not accounted for in trade models based solely on comparative advantage.

Exam Probability: **Medium**

14. *Answer choices:*

(see index for correct answer)

- a. Autarky
- b. current account
- c. Home market effect
- d. Gains from trade

Guidance: level 1

:: Social economy ::

_____ can be understood as the "third sector" of society, distinct from government and business, and including the family and the private sphere. By other authors, " _____ " is used in the sense of 1) the aggregate of non-governmental organizations and institutions that manifest interests and will of citizens or 2) individuals and organizations in a society which are independent of the government.

Exam Probability: **Low**

15. *Answer choices:*

(see index for correct answer)

- a. Social entrepreneurship
- b. Pozible
- c. Terminating deposit
- d. Benefit corporation

Guidance: level 1

:: Stock market ::

_____ is a term used in stock-trading to describe the practice of buying and selling shares or other securities without actually having the capital to cover the trade. In a cash account, a _____ violation occurs when the investor sells a stock that was purchased with unsettled funds.

Exam Probability: **Medium**

16. *Answer choices:*

(see index for correct answer)

- a. Free riding
- b. Bombay Stock Exchange
- c. Purple chip
- d. Tech Buzz

Guidance: level 1

:: Multinational companies ::

Abbott Medical Optics Inc. earlier known as _____ , Inc. is a global medical supply company. Products in the ophthalmic surgical line include intraocular lenses, laser vision correction systems, phacoemulsification systems, viscoelastics, microkeratomes and related products used in cataract and refractive surgery. AMO is based in Santa Ana, California, and employs approximately 4,200 worldwide. The company has operations in 24 countries and markets products in approximately 60 countries. In February 27, 2017, Abbott Medical Optics has changed its name to Johnson & Johnson Vision following its $4.3 billion acquisition by Johnson & Johnson.

Exam Probability: **Medium**

17. *Answer choices:*

(see index for correct answer)

- a. Cords Cable Industries Limited
- b. Gerdau

- c. TESCAN
- d. Advanced Medical Optics

Guidance: level 1

:: World economy ::

The _____ or global economy is the economy of the humans of the world, considered as the international exchange of goods and services that is expressed in monetary units of account. In some contexts, the two terms are distinct "international" or "global economy" being measured separately and distinguished from national economies while the " _____ " is simply an aggregate of the separate countries` measurements. Beyond the minimum standard concerning value in production, use and exchange the definitions, representations, models and valuations of the _____ vary widely. It is inseparable from the geography and ecology of Earth.

Exam Probability: **High**

18. *Answer choices:*
(see index for correct answer)

- a. Global workforce
- b. The World Economy

Guidance: level 1

:: International trade ::

A _____ , in international law, is a restraint on international trade or economic development to protect communities from development aggression or home industries from foreign competition.

Exam Probability: **Low**

19. *Answer choices:*

(see index for correct answer)

- a. Confirming house
- b. Offset agreement
- c. export-led growth
- d. International free trade agreement

Guidance: level 1

:: Income distribution ::

In economics, _____ is how a nation's total GDP is distributed amongst its population. Income and its distribution have always been a central concern of economic theory and economic policy. Classical economists such as Adam Smith, Thomas Malthus, and David Ricardo were mainly concerned with factor _____ , that is, the distribution of income between the main factors of production, land, labour and capital. Modern economists have also addressed this issue, but have been more concerned with the distribution of income across individuals and households. Important theoretical and policy concerns include the balance between income inequality and economic growth, and their often inverse relationship.

Exam Probability: **Medium**

20. *Answer choices:*

(see index for correct answer)

- a. Income distribution
- b. The rich get richer and the poor get poorer
- c. Guaranteed minimum income
- d. Redistributive justice

Guidance: level 1

:: International economics ::

In economics, _____ are the net benefits to economic agents from being allowed an increase in voluntary trading with each other. In technical terms, they are the increase of consumer surplus plus producer surplus from lower tariffs or otherwise liberalizing trade.

21. *Answer choices:*

(see index for correct answer)

- a. Eclectic paradigm
- b. Investment policy
- c. Multinational corporation
- d. Foreign Exchange Committee

Guidance: level 1

:: Trade routes ::

_____ involves the transfer of goods or services from one person or entity to another, often in exchange for money. A system or network that allows _____ is called a market.

Exam Probability: **Medium**

22. *Answer choices:*

(see index for correct answer)

- a. Caravan city
- b. Trade
- c. Salt road
- d. Camino de los chilenos

:: International development in Africa ::

_____ is an annual reference book-journal which focuses on the economics of most African countries. It reviews the recent economic situation and predicts the short-term interrelated economic, social, and political evolution of all African economies. The report is published by the OECD Development Centre, the African Development Bank, the United Nations Development Programme and United Nations Economic Commission for Africa. It was established in 2002.

Exam Probability: **Medium**

23. *Answer choices:*

(see index for correct answer)

- a. African Economic Outlook
- b. Village by Village
- c. Gatekeeper state
- d. Africa Progress Panel

:: Economic integration ::

An _____ is a type of trade bloc which is composed of a common market with a customs union. The participant countries have both common policies on product regulation, freedom of movement of goods, services and the factors of production and a common external trade policy. When an _____ involves unifying currency it becomes an economic and monetary union.

Exam Probability: **Medium**

24. *Answer choices:*

(see index for correct answer)

- a. Levant Union
- b. Economic union
- c. Economic partnership agreement
- d. Eurasian Economic Union

Guidance: level 1

:: International development in Africa ::

The _____ is chaired by the former Secretary-General of the United Nations and Nobel Laureate, Kofi Annan, and consists of the following members.

Exam Probability: **High**

25. *Answer choices:*

(see index for correct answer)

- a. AGETIP
- b. Village by Village
- c. African Growth and Opportunity Act
- d. Africa Progress Panel

Guidance: level 1

:: Economic indicators ::

The _____ , also known as balance of international payments and abbreviated B.O.P. or BoP, of a country is the record of all economic transactions between the residents of the country and the rest of the world in a particular period of time . These transactions are made by individuals, firms and government bodies. Thus the _____ includes all external visible and non-visible transactions of a country. It is an important issue to be studied, especially in international financial management field, for a few reasons.

Exam Probability: **Medium**

26. *Answer choices:*

(see index for correct answer)

- a. Balance of payments
- b. Travelex Confidence Index
- c. Net domestic product
- d. National Income and Product Accounts

:: International trade ::

_____ is a practice of employers to use cheaper labour than is usually available at their site of production or sale. In the latter case, migrant workers are employed; in the former, production is moved to a low-wage country or area. The company will thus save money and potentially increase its profit. Systemic criticism suggests that as a result, governments are tempted to enter a so-called social policy regime competition by reducing their labour and social standards to ease labour costs on enterprises and to retain business activity within their jurisdiction.

Exam Probability: **High**

27. *Answer choices:*

(see index for correct answer)

- a. Social dumping
- b. Standard trading conditions
- c. Theory of comparative advantage
- d. International Chamber of Commerce

:: International macroeconomics ::

The balance of trade, commercial balance, or _____ , is the difference between the monetary value of a nation's exports and imports over a certain time period. Sometimes a distinction is made between a balance of trade for goods versus one for services. The balance of trade measures a flow of exports and imports over a given period of time. The notion of the balance of trade does not mean that exports and imports are "in balance" with each other.

Exam Probability: **Low**

28. *Answer choices:*
(see index for correct answer)

- a. trade deficit
- b. Net exports
- c. Lucas paradox
- d. trade surplus

Guidance: level 1

:: Unemployment ::

_____ is a form of involuntary unemployment caused by a mismatch between the skills that workers in the economy can offer, and the skills demanded of workers by employers . _____ is often brought about by technological changes that make the job skills of many workers obsolete.

Exam Probability: **Low**

29. *Answer choices:*

(see index for correct answer)

- a. natural rate of unemployment
- b. Employment-population ratio
- c. Layoff
- d. Male unemployment

Guidance: level 1

:: Options (finance) ::

In finance, a put or put option is a stock market device which gives the owner the right, but not the obligation, to sell an asset , at a specified price , by a predetermined date to a given party . The purchase of a put option is interpreted as a negative sentiment about the future value of theunderlying stock. The term "put" comes from the fact that the owner has the right to "put up for sale" the stock or index.

Exam Probability: **Low**

30. *Answer choices:*

(see index for correct answer)

- a. Incentive stock option
- b. Contingent value rights
- c. Rainbow option
- d. Put options

:: Free trade agreements ::

The _____ is a free trade zone announced at the EAC-SADC-COMESA Summit on 22 October 2008 by the heads of Southern African Development Community , the Common Market for Eastern and Southern Africa and the East African Community . The _____ is also referred to as the African Free Trade Area in some official documents and press releases.

Exam Probability: **High**

31. *Answer choices:*

(see index for correct answer)

- a. South Asia Free Trade Agreement
- b. Asia-Pacific Trade Agreement
- c. African Free Trade Zone
- d. Central Asian Union

:: Economic Community of West African States ::

The _____ , also known as ECOWAS, is a regional economic union of fifteen countries located in West Africa. Collectively, these countries comprise an area of 5,114,162 km2 , and in 2015 had an estimated population of over 349 million.

Exam Probability: **High**

32. *Answer choices:*

(see index for correct answer)

- a. The Gambia
- b. Economic Community of West African States Monitoring Group
- c. Sierra Leone
- d. Burkina Faso

Guidance: level 1

:: International trade ::

The _____ is a plurilateral agreement under the auspices of the World Trade Organization that entered into force in 1981. It was then renegotiated in parallel with the Uruguay Round in 1994, and entered into force on 1 January 1996. The agreement was subsequently revised on 30 March 2012. The revised GPA came into effect on 6 July 2014. It regulates the government procurement of goods and services by the public authorities of the parties to the agreement, based on the principles of openness, transparency and non-discrimination.

Exam Probability: **Medium**

33. *Answer choices:*

(see index for correct answer)

- a. Trade mission
- b. International Centre for Trade and Sustainable Development
- c. Washington Consensus
- d. Agreement on Government Procurement

Guidance: level 1

:: Developing 8 Countries member states ::

_____ is a country in Southeast Asia. The federal constitutional monarchy consists of 13 states and three federal territories, separated by the South China Sea into two similarly sized regions, Peninsular _____ and East _____ . Peninsular _____ shares a land and maritime border with Thailand and maritime borders with Singapore, Vietnam, and Indonesia. East _____ shares land and maritime borders with Brunei and Indonesia and a maritime border with the Philippines and Vietnam. Kuala Lumpur is the national capital and largest city while Putrajaya is the seat of federal government. With a population of over 30 million, _____ is the world's 44th most populous country. The southernmost point of continental Eurasia, Tanjung Piai, is in _____ . In the tropics, _____ is one of 17 megadiverse countries, with large numbers of endemic species.

Exam Probability: **High**

34. *Answer choices:*

(see index for correct answer)

- a. Nigeria
- b. Pakistan
- c. Egypt
- d. Malaysia

Guidance: level 1

:: United States housing bubble ::

In economics, a _____ is a business cycle contraction when there is a general decline in economic activity. Macroeconomic indicators such as GDP , investment spending, capacity utilization, household income, business profits, and inflation fall, while bankruptcies and the unemployment rate rise. In the United Kingdom, it is defined as a negative economic growth for two consecutive quarters.

Exam Probability: **Low**

35. *Answer choices:*

(see index for correct answer)

- a. Constant maturity credit default swap
- b. United States housing bubble
- c. Recession
- d. Speculative fever

Guidance: level 1

:: Financial risk ::

_____ is a financial risk that for a certain period of time a given financial asset, security or commodity cannot be traded quickly enough in the market without impacting the market price.

Exam Probability: **Medium**

36. *Answer choices:*
(see index for correct answer)

- a. Spectral risk measure
- b. Credit risk
- c. Concentration risk
- d. Risk-adjusted return on capital

Guidance: level 1

:: International economics ::

_____ was an arrangement established in 1979 under the Jenkins European Commission where most nations of the European Economic Community linked their currencies to prevent large fluctuations relative to one another.

Exam Probability: **High**

37. *Answer choices:*

(see index for correct answer)

- a. Crawling peg
- b. Overshooting model
- c. European Monetary System
- d. Diamond model

Guidance: level 1

:: Trade policy ::

_____ is a trade policy that does not restrict imports or exports; it can also be understood as the free market idea applied to international trade. In government, _____ is predominantly advocated by political parties that hold liberal economic positions while economically left-wing and nationalist political parties generally support protectionism, the opposite of _____ .

Exam Probability: **Low**

38. *Answer choices:*

(see index for correct answer)

- a. Green box policies
- b. Free trade zone
- c. Enhanced integrated framework
- d. Free Trade

:: International trade ::

A _____ must be introduced when a group of countries forms a customs union. The same customs duties, import quotas, preferences or other non-tariff barriers to trade apply to all goods entering the area, regardless of which country within the area they are entering. It is designed to end re-exportation; but it may also inhibit imports from countries outside the customs union and thereby diminish consumer choice and support protectionism of industries based within the customs union. The _____ is a mild form of economic union but may lead to further types of economic integration. In addition to having the same customs duties, the countries may have other common trade policies, such as having the same quotas, preferences or other non-tariff trade regulations apply to all goods entering the area, regardless of which country, within the area, they are entering.

Exam Probability: **High**

39. *Answer choices:*

(see index for correct answer)

- a. Offshore outsourcing
- b. Trade agreement
- c. Common external tariff
- d. Development theory

:: International trade ::

An _____ is a good brought into a jurisdiction, especially across a national border, from an external source. The party bringing in the good is called an _____ er. An _____ in the receiving country is an export from the sending country. _____ ation and exportation are the defining financial transactions of international trade.

Exam Probability: **Low**

40. *Answer choices:*

(see index for correct answer)

- a. Cross-border cooperation
- b. Import license
- c. Most favoured nation
- d. International Coffee Agreement

Guidance: level 1

:: Commercial treaties ::

The _____ is a legal agreement between many countries, whose overall purpose was to promote international trade by reducing or eliminating trade barriers such as tariffs or quotas. According to its preamble, its purpose was the "substantial reduction of tariffs and other trade barriers and the elimination of preferences, on a reciprocal and mutually advantageous basis."

41. *Answer choices:*

(see index for correct answer)

- a. General Agreement on Tariffs and Trade
- b. Barcelona Convention and Statute on Freedom of Transit
- c. Methuen Treaty
- d. Treaty of Establishment, Commerce and Navigation

Guidance: level 1

:: Mortgage ::

A _____ is a mortgage loan, usually secured over a residential property, that enables the borrower to access the unencumbered value of the property. The loans are typically promoted to older homeowners and typically do not require monthly mortgage payments. Borrowers are still responsible for property taxes and homeowner's insurance. _____ s allow elders to access the home equity they have built up in their homes now, and defer payment of the loan until they die, sell, or move out of the home. Because there are no required mortgage payments on a _____ , the interest is added to the loan balance each month. The rising loan balance can eventually grow to exceed the value of the home, particularly in times of declining home values or if the borrower continues to live in the home for many years. However, the borrower is generally not required to repay any additional loan balance in excess of the value of the home.

42. *Answer choices:*

(see index for correct answer)

- a. Mortgage acceleration
- b. Reverse mortgage
- c. Warehouse line of credit
- d. Appraised value

Guidance: level 1

:: Dutch inventions ::

A central bank, reserve bank, or monetary authority is the institution that manages the currency, money supply, and interest rates of a state or formal monetary union,and oversees their commercial banking system. In contrast to a commercial bank, a central bank possesses a monopoly on increasing the monetary base in the state, and also generally controls the printing/coining of the national currency, which serves as the state's legal tender. A central bank also acts as a lender of last resort to the banking sector during times of financial crisis. Most _____ also have supervisory and regulatory powers to ensure the solvency of member institutions, to prevent bank runs, and to discourage reckless or fraudulent behavior by member banks.

Exam Probability: **Low**

43. *Answer choices:*

(see index for correct answer)

- a. Central banks

- b. Dutch gable
- c. Electrologica X8
- d. Fierljeppen

Guidance: level 1

:: Production economics ::

In microeconomics, _____ are the cost advantages that enterprises obtain due to their scale of operation , with cost per unit of output decreasing with increasing scale.

Exam Probability: **Medium**

44. *Answer choices:*
(see index for correct answer)

- a. Productivity Alpha
- b. HMI quality
- c. intermediate goods
- d. Production theory

Guidance: level 1

:: Economics curves ::

The _____ is the fraction of an increase in income that is not spent on an increase in consumption. That is, the _____ is the proportion of each additional dollar of household income that is used for saving. It is the slope of the line plotting saving against income. For example, if a household earns one extra dollar, and the _____ is 0.35, then of that dollar, the household will spend 65 cents and save 35 cents. Likewise, it is the fractional decrease in saving that results from a decrease in income.

Exam Probability: **Low**

45. *Answer choices:*

(see index for correct answer)

- a. J-curve
- b. Marginal propensity to save
- c. Phillips curve
- d. Hubbert curve

Guidance: level 1

:: Monetary policy ::

_____ is the loss of value of a country's currency with respect to one or more foreign reference currencies, typically in a floating exchange rate system in which no official currency value is maintained. Currency appreciation in the same context is an increase in the value of the currency. Short-term changes in the value of a currency are reflected in changes in the exchange rate.

46. *Answer choices:*

(see index for correct answer)

- a. Monetary policy
- b. Excess reserves
- c. Currency depreciation
- d. Impossible trinity

Guidance: level 1

:: Economics curves ::

The _____ is a single-equation econometric model, named after WilliamPhillips, describing a historical inverse relationship between rates of unemployment and corresponding rates of rises in wages that result within an economy. Stated simply, decreased unemployment, in an economy will correlate with higher rates of wage rises. Phillips did not himself state there was any relationship between employment and inflation; this notion was a trivial deduction from his statistical findings. Samuelson and Solow made the connection explicit and subsequently Milton Friedman and Edmund Phelpsput the theoretical structure in place. In so doing, Friedman was to successfully predict the imminent collapse of Phillips` a-theoretic correlation.

Exam Probability: **High**

47. *Answer choices:*

(see index for correct answer)

- a. Yield curve
- b. Phillips curve
- c. Kuznets curve
- d. Hubbert curve

Guidance: level 1

:: International trade ::

_____ is an economic term related to international economics in which trade is diverted from a more efficient exporter towards a less efficient one by the formation of a free trade agreement or a customs union. Total cost of good becomes cheaper when trading within the agreement because of the low tariff. This is as compared to trading with countries outside the agreement with lower cost goods but higher tariff. The related term Trade creation is when the formation of a trade agreement between countries decreases of price of the goods for more consumers, and therefore increases overall trade. In this case the more efficient producer with the agreement increases trade.

Exam Probability: **High**

48. *Answer choices:*
(see index for correct answer)

- a. Trade diversion
- b. Import license
- c. International Coffee Agreement
- d. Banyan merchants

:: Economics laws ::

The _____ states that in the absence of trade frictions , and under conditions of free competition and price flexibility , identical goods sold in different locations must sell for the same price when prices are expressed in a common currency. This law is derived from the assumption of the inevitable elimination of all arbitrage.

Exam Probability: **Low**

49. *Answer choices:*

(see index for correct answer)

- a. Law of increasing costs
- b. Walras' law
- c. Laws of costs
- d. Law of one price

:: Trade blocs ::

The _____ is an intergovernmental organization composed of six countries in the African Great Lakes region in eastern Africa: Burundi, Kenya, Rwanda, South Sudan, Tanzania, and Uganda. Paul Kagame, the president of Rwanda, is the EAC's chairman. The organisation was founded in 1967, collapsed in 1977, and was revived on 7 July 2000. In 2008, after negotiations with the Southern African Development Community and the Common Market for Eastern and Southern Africa , the EAC agreed to an expanded free trade area including the member states of all three organizations. The EAC is an integral part of the African Economic Community.

Exam Probability: **Medium**

50. *Answer choices:*

(see index for correct answer)

- a. Euro-Mediterranean free trade area
- b. East Asian Community
- c. Free Trade Area of the Americas
- d. East African Community

Guidance: level 1

:: International taxation ::

An _____ is an ahead-of-time agreement between a taxpayer and a tax authority on an appropriate transfer pricing methodology for a set of transactions at issue over a fixed period of time .

51. *Answer choices:*

(see index for correct answer)

- a. Currency transaction tax
- b. Double Irish arrangement
- c. Foreign housing exclusion
- d. Transfer pricing

Guidance: level 1

:: Taxation ::

Tax revenue is the income that is gained by governments through taxation. Taxation is the primary source of income for a state. Revenue may be extracted from sources such as individuals, public enterprises, trade, royalties on natural resources and/or foreign aid. An inefficient collection of taxes is greater in countries characterized by poverty, a large agricultural sector and large amounts of foreign aid.

Exam Probability: **Medium**

52. *Answer choices:*

(see index for correct answer)

- a. Deferred tax
- b. subsidies

- c. Tax holiday
- d. Tax revenues

Guidance: level 1

:: Constitutional state types ::

A _____ is a political entity characterized by a union of partially self-governing provinces, states, or other regions under a central federal government . In a _____ , the self-governing status of the component states, as well as the division of power between them and the central government, is typically constitutionally entrenched and may not be altered by a unilateral decision of either party, the states or the federal political body. Alternatively, _____ is a form of government in which sovereign power is formally divided between a central authority and a number of constituent regions so that each region retains some degree of control over its internal affairs. It is often argued that federal states where the central government has the constitutional authority to suspend a constituent state's government by invoking gross mismanagement or civil unrest, or to adopt national legislation that overrides or infringe on the constituent states' powers by invoking the central government's constitutional authority to ensure "peace and good government" or to implement obligations contracted under an international treaty, are not truly federal states.

Exam Probability: **Medium**

53. *Answer choices:*

(see index for correct answer)

- a. Federation
- b. Neutral territory

- c. Associated state
- d. Constituent country

Guidance: level 1

:: North American Free Trade Agreement ::

The _____ is an agreement signed by Canada, Mexico, and the United States, creating a trilateral trade bloc in North America. The agreement came into force on January 1, 1994, and superseded the 1988 Canada–United States Free Trade Agreement between the United States and Canada. The NAFTA trade bloc is one of the largest trade blocs in the world by gross domestic product.

Exam Probability: **Medium**

54. *Answer choices:*

(see index for correct answer)

- a. Commission for Environmental Cooperation
- b. Giant sucking sound
- c. Border Environment Cooperation Commission
- d. North American Agreement on Environmental Cooperation

Guidance: level 1

:: Sociocultural globalization ::

Human capital flight refers to the emigration of individuals who have received advanced training at home. The net benefits of human capital flight for the receiving country are sometimes referred to as a "brain gain" whereas the net costs for the sending country are sometimes referred to as a "_____". In occupations that experience a surplus of graduates, immigration of foreign-trained professionals can aggravate the underemployment of domestic graduates.

Exam Probability: **Medium**

55. *Answer choices:*

(see index for correct answer)

- a. Brain drain
- b. International organization
- c. World population
- d. Democratization of technology

Guidance: level 1

:: International trade ::

An _____ is a type of trade restriction that sets a physical limit on the quantity of a good that can be imported into a country in a given period of time.

Exam Probability: **Medium**

56. *Answer choices:*

(see index for correct answer)

- a. Hilton Quota
- b. New Zealand Dairy Board
- c. Walvis Bay Export Processing Zone
- d. Import quota

Guidance: level 1

:: Free market ::

_____ is the act of buyers and sellers freely and willingly engaging in market transactions. Moreover, transactions are made in such a way that both the buyer and the seller are better off after the exchange than before it occurred.

Exam Probability: **Medium**

57. *Answer choices:*

(see index for correct answer)

- a. Voluntary exchange
- b. White market
- c. Free market
- d. Henry Hazlitt Foundation

:: Financial markets ::

As money became a commodity, the _____ became a component of the financial market for assets involved in short-term borrowing, lending, buying and selling with original maturities of one year or less. Trading in _____ s is done over the counter and is wholesale.

Exam Probability: **Low**

58. *Answer choices:*

(see index for correct answer)

- a. Money market
- b. Layering
- c. Thomson Reuters league tables
- d. Forex signal

:: Economic indicators ::

_____ is a way of measuring economic variables in different countries so that irrelevant exchange rate variations do not distort comparisons. Purchasing power exchange rates are such that it would cost exactly the same number of, for example, US dollars to buy euros and then buy a basket of goods in the market as it would cost to purchase the same goods directly with dollars. The purchasing power exchange rate used in this conversion equals the ratio of the currencies` respective purchasing powers .

Exam Probability: **Low**

59. *Answer choices:*

(see index for correct answer)

- a. Purchasing power parity
- b. Magazine cover indicator
- c. Consumer leverage ratio
- d. Misery index

Guidance: level 1

INDEX: Correct Answers

Introduction to economics

1. c: Economic model

2. d: Security

3. b: Asset

4. c: Cartel

5. a: Great Depression

6. b: Monopolistic competition

7. d: Nominal interest rate

8. a: Communism

9. c: Diminishing returns

10. a: Tax cut

11. d: Stock

12. b: Law of supply

13. a: Demand

14. a: Export

15. b: Exchange rate

16. b: Google

17. c: Retained earnings

18. c: Cash

19. b: Present value

20. : Theory

21. a: Moral hazard

22. a: Credit

23. : GDP deflator

24. d: Income elasticity of demand

25. d: Economic policy

26. c: Earned income

27. c: Public policy

28. c: Stagflation

29. : Competition

30. : Price level

31. c: Wage

32. c: Industrial Revolution

33. d: International Trade

34. d: Internet

35. b: Trade deficit

36. a: Hypothesis

37. d: Circular flow

38. a: Income distribution

39. d: Preference

40. a: Recession

41. d: Rational expectations

42. b: Supply shock

43. : Cost curve

44. d: Political economy

45. : Euro

46. c: Technological change

47. b: Keynesian economics

48. a: Structural unemployment

49. c: Marginal cost

50. : Deflation

51. : Tax credit

52. d: Aggregate demand

53. : Economies of scale

54. b: Saving

55. b: Protectionism

56. a: Capitalism

57. c: Real wage

58. a: Money multiplier

59. d: Tariff

Fundamental economics

1. : Keynesian economics

2. c: Advertising

3. c: Game theory

4. : Consumer price index

5. c: Monetary policy

6. : Gross domestic product

7. b: Price level

8. d: Moral hazard

9. d: Asset

10. c: Rationing

11. a: Problem

12. c: Aggregate demand

13. : Mining

14. a: Initial public offering

15. b: Microeconomics

16. a: Market value

17. c: Schedule

18. d: Devaluation

19. c: Comparative advantage

20. d: Sustainability

21. c: World Trade Organization

22. d: Perfect competition

23. d: Barriers to entry

24. : Fixed cost

25. d: Private property

26. b: Interest rate

27. c: Full employment

28. b: Income

29. a: Foreign direct investment

30. c: Barter

31. c: Government spending

32. b: Bank

33. b: Good

34. a: Excess reserves

35. : Bailout

36. : Theory

37. d: Deflator

38. a: Baby Boomers

39. d: Money market

40. : Dividend

41. d: Security

42. a: Productive efficiency

43. c: Inflation targeting

44. a: Classical economics

45. c: Federal Reserve Bank

46. b: Business cycle

47. c: Property

48. b: New Deal

49. b: Balance sheet

50. b: Income distribution

51. : Financial capital

52. a: Aggregate supply

53. d: Marginal cost

54. c: Economic policy

55. : Demand curve

56. b: Hyperinflation

57. c: Discouraged worker

58. d: Competition

59. b: Macroeconomics

Mathematical and quantitative methods

1. c: Determinant

2. c: Venn diagram

3. d: Face validity

4. c: Two-way analysis of variance

5. c: Probability distribution

6. : Injective

7. c: Risk management

8. c: Hicksian demand

9. c: Moving-average model

10. d: Total sum of squares

11. : Frequency

12. : External validity

13. : Z-test

14. c: Standard deviation

15. d: Portmanteau test

16. d: Base period

17. : Population model

18. : Inverse demand function

19. d: Seasonal adjustment

20. b: Sampling distribution

21. a: Metadata

22. : Shadow price

23. d: Expected return

24. c: Central tendency

25. c: Scatter plot

26. b: Economic development

27. b: Gaussian elimination

28. d: Interval estimation

29. a: Studentized range

30. a: Stem-and-leaf display

31. d: Minitab

32. d: Pie chart

33. a: Internal validity

34. c: Exponential smoothing

35. a: Normal probability plot

36. b: Prior probability

37. c: Time series

38. c: Overfitting

39. d: Econometrica

40. d: Statistical significance

41. : Price index

42. c: Grouped data

43. b: Surjective

44. a: Census

45. c: Lower bound

46. : Code

47. : Choropleth map

48. b: Seasonality

49. d: Market risk

50. c: One-way analysis of variance

51. b: Present value

52. b: Unstructured data

53. : Vector measure

54. c: Nonparametric regression

55. c: Operational

56. : Objective function

57. b: Bayesian statistics

58. d: U-statistic

59. a: Expenditure function

Microeconomics

1. a: Adverse selection

2. a: Economic model

3. a: Great Recession

4. : Income effect

5. d: Progressive tax

6. a: Externality

7. a: Minimum wage law

8. c: Excess burden

9. c: Diminishing marginal return

10. d: Negative income tax

11. d: Economies of scope

12. b: Kinked demand

13. c: Demand schedule

14. c: Interest

15. a: Returns to scale

16. a: Long run

17. b: Policy

18. c: Price controls

19. a: Physical capital

20. b: Industrial policy

21. c: Welfare reform

22. a: Tax incidence

23. : Energy economics

24. d: Residual claimant

25. a: Market share

26. b: Shareholder

27. : Consumer sovereignty

28. : Recession

29. b: Comparative statics

30. d: Economic efficiency

31. c: Minimum wage

32. a: Welfare economics

33. c: Resource allocation

34. d: Credit

35. : Auction

36. a: Government intervention

37. a: Inflation

38. : Variable cost

39. d: Renewable resource

40. d: Saving

41. b: Stock

42. b: Income

43. a: Competitive equilibrium

44. c: Inferior good

45. c: Marginal product

46. c: Productivity

47. a: Bankruptcy

48. b: External cost

49. d: Factor price

50. : Deductible

51. c: Retirement

52. d: Short run

53. : Sunk costs

54. : Black market

55. b: Deadweight loss

56. c: Monopoly

57. c: Elasticity of demand

58. c: Total revenue

59. a: Wage

Macroeconomics and monetary economics

1. c: Inventory

2. a: Real interest rate

3. c: Structural unemployment

4. a: Mutual fund

5. c: Law of supply

6. a: Financial market

7. b: Central bank

8. c: Inventory investment

9. a: Money

10. a: Stock market

11. a: Natural rate of unemployment

12. d: Export

13. b: Economic development

14. : Purchasing power

15. : Supply and demand

16. a: Credit

17. b: Good

18. : Transaction cost

19. a: Unemployment

20. c: Law of one price

21. : Business cycle

22. : Commodity money

23. c: Recessionary gap

24. b: Marginal propensity to consume

25. a: Nominal GDP

26. c: Short run

27. c: Capitalism

28. : Wage

29. d: Current account

30. b: Underground economy

31. : Outsourcing

32. b: Household

33. : Government spending

34. b: Finance

35. c: Inflationary gap

36. a: Free trade

37. d: Unit of account

38. b: Demand schedule

39. a: Product market

40. b: Physical capital

41. b: Price

42. c: Hyperinflation

43. c: International trade

44. d: Transfer payment

45. b: Great Moderation

46. c: Fiat money

47. : Law of demand

48. a: Automatic stabilizer

49. a: Capital good

50. a: Bond market

51. d: Policy

52. c: Private property

53. : Recession

54. b: Time deposit

55. b: Adaptive expectations

56. d: Income tax

57. b: Federal Reserve Bank

58. : Income distribution

59. b: Economic recovery

Business economics

1. d: Perfect competition

2. a: Yield curve

3. : Transaction cost

4. d: Washington Mutual

5. : Commercial paper

6. d: Probability distribution

7. d: Dental insurance

8. d: Bear spread

9. a: Economic rent

10. b: Asset specificity

11. a: Arc elasticity

12. b: Barter

13. d: Citigroup

14. b: Devaluation

15. b: Lehman Brothers

16. b: Rationing

17. a: Free trade

18. c: Dividend policy

19. : Leveraged buyout

20. d: Private equity

21. b: Marginal cost

22. d: Financial market

23. a: Transfer pricing

24. d: Net present value

25. b: Capital asset pricing model

26. : Capital budgeting

27. a: Relative price

28. : Market share

29. c: Derived demand

30. : OPEC

31. a: Bull spread

32. a: Operating leverage

33. : Price

34. a: Effective exchange rate index

35. d: Netflix

36. d: Liberalization

37. b: Public good

38. a: Dividend

39. c: Debt ratio

40. : Selling

41. a: Double taxation

42. a: Barings Bank

43. d: RAND Health Insurance Experiment

44. : Return on assets

45. d: Advertising

46. d: Stock exchange

47. a: Asset turnover

48. d: Asset

49. d: Expected return

50. d: Auditor independence

51. : Empirical evidence

52. c: Bank run

53. c: Internal rate of return

54. a: Cost-effectiveness analysis

55. c: Risk premium

56. b: Globalization

57. b: Market clearing

58. b: Need

59. c: Moral hazard

International economics

1. c: Gold standard

2. : Indonesia

3. d: Horizontal integration

4. : Countervailing duties

5. b: Forward market

6. : Free trade area

7. : Autarky

8. c: OPEC

9. d: 1970s energy crisis

10. a: Chiang Mai Initiative

11. b: Market risk

12. c: Tax rate

13. : General equilibrium

14. c: Home market effect

15. : Civil society

16. a: Free riding

17. d: Advanced Medical Optics

18. c: World economy

19. : Safeguard

20. a: Income distribution

21. : Gains from trade

22. b: Trade

23. a: African Economic Outlook

24. b: Economic union

25. d: Africa Progress Panel

26. a: Balance of payments

27. a: Social dumping

28. b: Net exports

29. : Structural unemployment

30. d: Put options

31. c: African Free Trade Zone

32. : Economic Community of West African States

33. d: Agreement on Government Procurement

34. d: Malaysia

35. c: Recession

36. : Liquidity risk

37. c: European Monetary System

38. d: Free Trade

39. c: Common external tariff

40. : Import

41. a: General Agreement on Tariffs and Trade

42. b: Reverse mortgage

43. a: Central banks

44. : Economies of scale

45. b: Marginal propensity to save

46. c: Currency depreciation

47. b: Phillips curve

48. a: Trade diversion

49. d: Law of one price

50. d: East African Community

51. : Advance pricing agreement

52. d: Tax revenues

53. a: Federation

54. : North American Free Trade Agreement

55. a: Brain drain

56. d: Import quota

57. a: Voluntary exchange

58. a: Money market

59. a: Purchasing power parity

CPSIA information can be obtained
at www.ICGtesting.com
Printed in the USA
LVHW051628301019
635718LV00005B/621/P